CIGAR BOX BANJO

PAUL QUARRINGTON

NOTES ON MUSIC AND LIFE

BOX
BANJO

GREYSTONE BOOKS
D&M PUBLISHERS INC.
Vancouver/Toronto/Berkeley

Greystone Books
An imprint of D&M Publishers Inc.
2323 Quebec Street, Suite 201
Vancouver BC Canada V5T 4S7
www.greystonebooks.com

Cataloguing data available from Library and Archives Canada

ISBN 978-1-55365-438-4 (cloth)
ISBN 978-1-55365-629-6 (ebook)

Editing by Barbara Pulling
Copy editing by Peter Norman
Jacket design by Heather Pringle
Text design by Jessica Sullivan

"Hello Jim" © Paul Quarrington/Cordova Bay Music Publishing;
"Are You Ready" © If Dreams Had Wings Music/Cordova Bay Music Publishing

Printed and bound in Canada by Friesens
Text printed on 100% post-consumer, acid-free paper
Distributed in the U.S. by Publishers Group West

We gratefully acknowledge the financial support of the Canada
Council for the Arts, the British Columbia Arts Council, the Province of
British Columbia through the Book Publishing Tax Credit, and the Government
of Canada through the Canada Book Fund for our publishing activities.

Mixed Sources
Cert no. SW-COC-001271
© 1996 FSC
FSC

FOREWORD

As I start to write this I'm listening to an album called *You & Me*, by a band called the Walkmen. Ten minutes ago, I bought an album called *Songs of Shame*, by a band called Woods. I did this so I'd have something new on my iPod as I walk to collect my daughter from her choir practice later today. Last night I volunteered to wash the dishes because a) the dishwasher is broken, and b) I could listen to four or five tracks from another recent purchase, the Velvet Underground's *Loaded*. Actually, it's *Fully Loaded*, which is *Loaded* with extras, including a demo version of "Satellite of Love," a song that became famous later in Lou Reed's career. The final version, the version I first listened to in 1973, is on Reed's album *Transformer*. I still remember loving the lines:

> I've been told that you've been bold
> With Harry, Mark, and John.

I remember hoping that my parents would—and wouldn't—charge in from the room next door and demand that I stop playing the record. The record didn't belong to me. I had it for the night and I was recording it by holding my tape recorder up to one of the stereo speakers. The whole record was a taunt, to me, to my parents, to the world. But they didn't charge in; they remained untaunted. Nevertheless, I've always loved those lines.

The demo on *Fully Loaded* was recorded in 1970 and the lyrics are slightly, but significantly, different.

I've been told that you've been bold
With Wynken, Blynken, and Nod.

The "Wynken, Blynken" version was recorded two years before "Harry, Mark, and John" but my reaction, when I heard "Wynken" and "Blynken" last night, was almost violent. What did Reed think he was doing? I know: he'd actually changed the lyrics and saved the day. And I know: it's only a couple of lines from a song. But, for a few seconds, the time it took to wash one bowl and overcome the urge to smash it, I couldn't see that. To claim that music is more important than oxygen would be trite and sentimental. But it would also be true.

I love music. I seem to remember a disco song with those words—*I love music, any kind of music*. I just looked it up; it was the O'Jays. I wouldn't be as generous as the O'Jays, because I think most music is shite. But I have to admit, if I'd been in the O'Jays—and I wish I had been—I'd have been quite content to sing along. *I love music, even shite music.* Which is just as well, because I live on an island called Ireland where much of the music is shite. I grew up listening to "Danny Boy"; I grew up hating Danny Boy, and all his siblings and his granny. *The pipes, the pipes are caw-haw-haw-hawling.* Anything with pipes or fiddles or even—forgive me, Paul—banjos, I detested. Songs of loss, of love or land; songs of flight and emigration, of going across the sea; songs of defiance and rebellion—I vomited on all of them. My own act of rebellion, in a wet land full of rebel songs, was to hate all Irish rebel songs, in fact, all Irish songs, everything that sounded vaguely Irish, including the language and all who spoke it, or even thought in it.

Then I heard Jackie Wilson singing "Danny Boy." It wasn't that his rendition was extraordinary, although it is. The song just stopped being Irish. It was being sung—it was being demolished—by Jackie Wilson, a black American who, as far as I knew, had no connection with Ireland, and I could actually listen to the song. It was a liberating, interesting moment. Liberating, because, freed of its time and geography, it became a song that I could like. Interesting, because it made me think about songs in general and what made them good, or bad. "I Say a Little Prayer" is my favourite song, but only if it's sung by Aretha Franklin. "When Irish Eyes Are Smiling" is a dreadful song, but I wish Otis Redding had recorded it. I'd never liked "The Rocky Road to Dublin," another of the songs I was unable to avoid when I was a child, until I heard and saw it used at the end of a documentary film called *Rocky Road to Dublin*. The film was made in Dublin, in 1967. The camera is on the back of a lorry as it passes a school, very like the school I went to, just as the school is emptying. The boys, very like the boys I knew and the boy I'd been, spot the camera and run after it. That's what you see as the Dubliners start to play and Luke Kelly starts to sing, the boys charging after the lorry. It's an exhilarating end to what is a brilliant, but depressing, film about the misery of life in Ireland in 1967. These boys cheerfully running after the lorry become the country's future, the children who'll grow up and rescue the place. And the song, a song about emigration written sometime in the nineteenth century—*saluted father dear, kissed my darlin' mother, drank a pint of beer, my grief and tears to smother*—becomes the rhythm of that future. One of the songs I'd taught myself to hate became wonderful—even with the banjo.

Why am I writing all this? (By the way, I'm listening to Grizzly Bear now.) I suppose it's to suggest that I'm qualified to write the foreword to a book about songs. I've never written a song, or a line from a song. I've met people who think I wrote the soundtrack to *The Commitments* and, once or twice, I haven't put them right. I have to admit, it's nice being the man who wrote "Mustang Sally." But I know: I didn't write "Mustang Sally," or "Try A Little Tenderness." I currently have 4,920 songs on my iPod, and I wrote none of them. But I love all of them. I love yapping about songs and their composers and interpreters, probably more than actually listening to them. My books are full of songs. Subtract the song lyrics and one or two of my novels would immediately become short stories. So, I'm qualified.

But that's not why I was delighted to be asked to write this foreword. I wanted to do it because I wanted Paul Quarrington to read it.

I have friends I grew up with, and friends I've met along the way. Paul Quarrington is one of the latter. If I try, I can calculate the number of times I've met him. All I have to do is work out the number of times I've visited Toronto, add a trip to Calgary and a few meetings in New York. It might be ten, or nine, or thirteen. But it doesn't feel like that. I met a friend of Paul's recently and I assumed, because of the way he spoke about Paul, the obvious affection that was there, that he'd known Paul for years, decades, significant chunks of two centuries. But I found out later that they'd met less than a year before. It didn't really surprise me. Ten minutes in the company of Paul Quarrington, and you're instantly an old friend. It feels like that and—I don't know how—it *is* like that.

So, I can claim, if only to myself, to be an old friend of Paul's. And I can claim to be an admirer of his work, because it's true. I think *Whale Music* is magnificent. Or, if I had to restrict "magnificent" to just one book, I'd give it to *Civilization* and declare *Whale Music* "an inch short of magnificent."

At this point I stopped writing the foreword.

I went to India, to attend the Jaipur Literature Festival. It took me a day and a half to get there. I had to leave Dublin earlier than I'd planned, to avoid a strike by Dublin's air traffic controllers. At the other end, the journey from Delhi airport to Jaipur was a seven-hour terror, as the driver slalomed between trucks and camels, off the road, back on the road, around sacred cows and through crowds of people, past rows of elephants, thumping the horn and muttering to himself all the way. When I finally got to the hotel, I slid onto the bed and slept like an unhappy baby, my body on the bed, my head still in the car. But my head eventually stopped, and I slept properly. I woke the next morning, happy to be in India for the first time. I plugged in my laptop and checked my e-mail. There was far more incoming mail than was usual, most of it from friends and acquaintances in Canada, and the subject lines on all of them—*Paul, Paul Q, Paul Quarrington*—told me that Paul had died. I felt very far from home.

I answered most of the e-mails and texted my wife, Belinda. She phoned later. (There's a five-and-a-half-hour time difference between Jaipur and Dublin.) By that time I was at the festival, and I cried a bit as I spoke to her. She'd never met Paul but she knew how highly I regarded him. (Writing about Paul in the past tense feels like betrayal.) I always came home from Toronto with new Paul stories; he was always on his way to Dublin.

Belinda never met Paul but it was through her that I met him. She'd worked in a college in Dublin some time in the mid-1980s when a young man from Toronto called Dave Bidini came visiting. They became friends. He stayed a summer, I think, then went back home to Canada—and Ireland breathed a giddy sigh of relief. Years later, he wrote to her, with the news that he was coming to Dublin with his band, the Rheostatics, and that they all loved a book called *The Commitments*. She wrote back with the news that she was married to the man who wrote *The Commitments*. So, I met Dave—another instant old friend. He introduced me to Paul.

I cried, a bit, as I spoke to Belinda on my mobile phone, in a quiet corner, perhaps the only quiet corner in Jaipur. I told her how I'd hoped that Paul would read the foreword, that he'd read how much I admired his work and how much I admired him, how much I just plain liked him and loved him. But, even as I spoke, I knew: Paul had always known that. He'd have seen it on my face every time we met. What made me cry was the obvious, stupid fact that we'd never meet again.

I had a great time in Jaipur. I thought about Paul a lot. He'd have loved the cows. On the way back to Delhi, in a fog as thick as old milk, the car I was in nearly—really very fuckin' nearly—crashed into the back of a stationary truck. In the split second before I died—I was calm, terrified, certain of this—I didn't think of Paul at all. There were no nice thoughts of the bar in heaven, where Paul would be waiting, with a cold beer for me; or thoughts of the bar in hell, where Paul would be waiting, with a warm beer for me—and a banjo. An eternity of warm beer I could tolerate, even enjoy. But an eternity of the banjo? Even un-strummed, it would be torture, squatting there waiting to be strummed.

But the brakes worked, finally, and I didn't die. I survived, and so did my atheism. Paul is dead.

But how he died. It's in this book. A book about music becomes a book about music and death, and Paul manages to make them hold hands. (When considering Paul's work, I can use the present tense and it feels like honesty.) A hugely enjoyable, very funny book about Paul's career in music becomes a magnificent book about his death and remains hugely enjoyable and very funny—in fact, funnier. He saw it coming and he took control.

Paul died. But, as this book so brilliantly reveals, and as those of us who are so, so lucky to have known him and to have been known by him understand—in all possible meanings of the word—Paul *lived*.

RODDY DOYLE

INTRODUCTION

AT THE beginning of 2009, I completed a draft of a book I was calling *The Song*. It was a slim volume that dovetailed my involvement in music (I am assiduously avoiding the word "career") with a look at some songs I felt were noteworthy and influential: "This Land Is Your Land," "Like a Rolling Stone," the enigmatic "Pancho and Lefty." The Publisher quite liked the draft—"Some fine writing here," he said, "some of your best"—but there were problems. Apparently, when I attempted musicology, things flattened out some. My attempts to explain the intricacies of chord theory were confusing. "But," said the Publisher, "the personal stuff is great. You learning to play the guitar, those groups with your brother, then all the songwriting stuff, the stories about Martin, Joe Hall, Dan Hill, Dan Lanois[1]..."

---

[1] I actually have nothing more to say about Mr. Lanois at this moment. I just wanted to introduce the notion of footnotes, and I thought his name afforded a good opportunity to get people to glance downwards. Thank you.

All right. It's good that the Publisher liked the personal stuff, because...

In the early spring, as soon as the weather turned at all nice, I had my racing bike refitted and took to the streets. Actually, I took to the paths that wend their way beside the ravines in our fair city of Toronto. I bicycled into Wilket Creek Park (past the pond that features in both my non-fiction book *The Boy on the Back of the Turtle* and my novel *The Ravine*) and ventured up a steep hill that the year before I had been able to climb with—well, not ease, but I'd been able to do it. Halfway up, I abandoned the bike, gasping for breath. Moreover, I was panicking, part of me not believing that I would ever intake the amount of air needed for resuscitation. "I," I told myself, "am in pretty bad shape." So the next day I embarked on a program of brisk walking, largely in a nearby cemetery with a hill that had historically winded me. I would walk up the hill and then gasp for breath as I continued down the roadway, checking my progress against whichever stone marker happened to be alongside when I resumed breathing reasonably comfortably. I tended to end up beside my favourite gravestone. It had been erected for a man named John Ivan Johnson, and there was an etching of a racehorse beside his name. Underneath were the cryptic words "Just by a Nose."

Sometimes, though, I found myself beside this marker with no lessening of the gasping. "Hmm," I told myself, "perhaps something is wrong." I Googled my symptoms and came up with a long list of possibilities, including the somewhat rare "vocal cord disorder," as I had had, over the previous months, some issues with my singing voice. (And I am a singer, you understand: I sing with the group Porkbelly Futures and play the rhythm guitar, although the actual rhythm section, the lads on the battery of drums and bass, might quibble with that designation.) So I went to my doctor, suggesting this iffy self-diagnosis, and he checked my throat and nose and diagnosed "post nasal drip," which had infected my vocal cords. I liked this diagnosis, although some inner part of me cautioned that he hadn't eliminated any of the really dire possibilities.

Things worsened. I often found myself beside the "Just by a Nose" gravestone still sucking in huge quaffs of air. "I," I told myself, "am asthmatic. Or else allergic to something. Air, for example."

The first weekend of May, I was scheduled to make a couple of appearances in Ottawa, Ontario. I had been invited to speak at a symposium on the Friday evening, and on Sunday I was giving a house concert. I drove up to Ottawa, checked into a rather nice hotel, and, as soon as I stepped outside, noticed I was having much more trouble breathing. Even a little rise, hardly apparent in the landscape, would have me inhaling heavily. I went back and put in some time on the stationary bike in the hotel workout room. I set the machine at a low level—two, I think, perhaps one—but I managed to get through about fifty minutes without too much stress. Thus, when I walked outside only to be rendered windless once more, I came to the sole conclusion an intelligent, right-thinking man could: I had an *extreme allergic reaction to tulips*. After all, Ottawa's famous Canadian Tulip Festival was in full swing, and those fucking bulbs were sending up blossoms everywhere.

The symposium, at the University of Ottawa, was about film and literature. My talk was the keynote address, as one of my novels—*Whale Music*—had been made into a fine motion picture by Richard J. Lewis. Indeed, I might mention, given the intended purview of this book, that my biggest success to that point as a songwriter had arisen out of that film. The film's soundtrack was created by the Toronto indie rock band the Rheostatics, and the script called for the main character, Desmond Howl, to write a song. He is inspired by a young woman named Claire, and I suggest, in the book and the movie script, some lines that might come to him: "Purify me, purify me, Claire." The Rheostatics took these words and expanded upon them, and when the song "Claire" was done I was listed as one of the writers. "Claire" went on to win a Genie award (that's the Canadian version of the Oscar, or so we Canadians like to aver) and subsequently got quite a bit of airplay.

I made it through my address—I had to clip quite a few sentences, chop them up into tiny aspirated phrases—then went to the hospitality suite of the Ottawa Writers Festival. Hey, it was in my hotel. I stayed quite late and got drunk with festival fun-guy rob mclennan and some of his colleagues, sound poets jw curry, Max Middle, and Carmel Purkis. The poets performed some of their stuff in the wee hours of the morning, emitting strange inhuman noises.

The next day—after an inexplicably exhausting journey to the store to purchase some medications (Buckley's Cough Mixture and lozenges for my croaking throat, a big bottle of Tums for a certain sloshing heaviness I felt about my gut)—I drove out to Chelsea to visit my brother Joel. Also in attendance was Robert Wilson, who is the manager/booking agent for Porkbelly Futures. We barbecued many kinds of meat and drank many bottles of wine, so when I lay down to sleep and found comfort an impossibility, I had no reason for undue concern.

Now, I know you people out there are observing a certain irritating disregard for reality on my part, an ability for self-deception that would rival a three-year-old's. For what it's worth, over breakfast I did instruct Joel to Google many ailments: the aforementioned "vocal cord disorder," "pneumonia," "pleurisy," and, yeah, "lung cancer." But we ruled out lung cancer because a) I had not been coughing up blood and b) I had not experienced a "sudden and unexplained weight loss." I drove back to the hotel.

The following day was the house concert. In case you are unfamiliar with this concept, I was, essentially, going to sing in someone's living room. The people who were invited paid a small entrance fee, and the money would all be turned over to me. Interestingly, the woman who invited me, Renate Mohr, was someone I had known as a child. Her father, Hans, and my father were colleagues, and every so often their family would visit. Renate's nickname all those years ago had been Tutti, which is how I addressed her. "Tutti," I said when I arrived, "this is Carmel." Yes, I had conscripted one of the sound poets from the Hospitality Suite to drive me, because, as I explained to Tutti, "I think in order to do this I'm going to have to get pretty drunk." I had a bottle of whisky with me, I had my Buckley's, and I hoped that the combo would loosen up the vocal cords and give me the requisite energy. It worked out pretty well. I sang some songs, and I read some poetry.

It occurs to me that I might add one of those poems into these very pages. After all, it has a thematic connection, and it includes a suitably dramatic bit of foreshadowing.

Crossroad Blues

When I was 15
My mother died and I
Started playing the blues on
A Zenon guitar and
Drinking Four Aces wine,
Which was not really wine.

Just like Robert Johnson.
Who made a deal with the Devil
at the Crossroads.
Robert Johnson sold his Soul
To the Devil,
Which was like selling his shoes
When he knew he had to walk down
A road of horseshoe nails.

I would listen to the records
And learn the licks with
Tongue-biting concentration.

I was pale and chubby and little-dicked.
I would drink Four Aces,
Which was not really wine,
But it was alcohol.
I would play the guitar,
Drunk in my bedroom,
Hiding from my father,
Who was drunk in the den

Of our house in Don Mills, Ontario,
Canada's first planned community.

One night the Devil
Appeared in my bedroom.
The Devil has some personal hygiene issues
Which we need not get into.

The Devil offered me the same deal
He offered Robert Johnson
At the Crossroads.

He said, "I will make you
The best guitar player ever.
You will make strong men cry
And you will make women wilt
With their desire for you.
The songs you write will haunt
Mankind forever.
It will cost you your Soul."

I thought about it.

"Well . . . what would it cost
If you just showed me how to play
An F7?"

Afterwards, Carmel drove me back downtown; we parked
the car and went out for a drink and a bite. I didn't eat much,
despite having not eaten much all day. Indeed, it was perhaps

the only time in my life when a female dining companion was given the opportunity to point to the remaining eighth of quesadilla on my plate and say, "Are you gonna eat that? Because…" I didn't eat much, but I drank some. Then we walked out onto the street, sat down on a bench and Carmel—whom, I should mention, is a very attractive young woman—said, "I guess I'll grab a cab."

"You could always spend the night with me at the hotel."

Carmel cast her eyes downward. "I don't think that would be such a good idea. You see—"

"Okay." I kissed her and put her in a cab. As I stumbled away into the night, only then was it impressed upon me that, indeed, something was very, very wrong.

HAVING GIVEN a rasping, panting house concert in Ottawa, having delivered a half-assed pass and then not worried one bit when it was deflected, I drove back to Toronto the next day. I felt reasonably fine, although my hands kept seizing up, the muscles constricting, so I could keep only one on the steering wheel at a time, the other requiring stretching and bending. I was scheduled to go out to dinner with an old flame, and when she called me at home in the middle of the afternoon, I reiterated my intention of supping with her. Roseanne listened to me for a little less than a minute. "Paul," she said, "stay right there. I'm coming to take you to the hospital."

"All right." I had already considered going to the hospital, you see. I packed a bag, including a night kit and a book. Then I added another book, because I entertained, very vaguely, the idea that I wouldn't be coming out for a long time.

The emergency triage nurse put a stethoscope to my back to listen to my breathing. She called over a nearby paramedic.

"I can't find the left lung," the nurse said. The paramedic announced that she could hear it, albeit very faintly. "Don't worry," she told me, "it's there." If you want to be hustled over the hurdles in an emergency ward, it's a good idea to have something very wrong with you. In no time I was sitting on a hospital bed, dressed in the undignified backless Johnny shirt.

I was wheeled down to X-Ray, where a nice young man rendered an image of my innards, blasting the rays through my back. "Just wait here," he said, ducking through the door, "until I make sure I have it." A second later he called, "Paul! What have you done?"

"What do you mean?"

"I mean ... they're going to want to keep you here, I think."[2]

Back in my emergency cubicle, I waited. The woman in the cubicle next door wouldn't lie on her bed, choosing to curl up on the floor and call out loudly for drugs. After some time, a young physician came in and reported that a lot of fluid had accumulated around my lungs. "We'll try to get rid of some of it," he said, "so you'll be more comfortable. Then we'll try to figure out why it's there."

"Okay." I didn't call anyone. I didn't want to alarm people, I suppose, and at that moment, I couldn't really think of anyone to alarm. My most recent romantic relationship had busted up. I had an ex-wife, one adult daughter (the other still a teen), friends I figured would come to my aid. But, hell, it was probably just pneumonia, exacerbated by my severe tulip allergy.

When a new doctor, Dr. Tran, came in, he informed me that there were many reasons I might have fluid around

---

2 I learned later the technician was reacting to the fact that when he checked the X-ray, there was only a huge white cloud where the left lung should have appeared.

my lungs, the most common two being infection and cancer. "Infection is eight times more common than cancer," he
said. He left, then returned a short while later with a tray
full of equipment, vials and litre bottles and lengths of tubing and assorted needles. He and an aide made me sit up on
my wheelie hospital bed. They placed a table beside it so that
I could drape my arms across it and lean forward. Dr. Tran
tapped and thumped my back with his thick fingers, marked
a spot with a pirate's X for freezing. "Little sting like a bee," he
said as the needle carrying the anaesthetic pierced the skin.
He didn't say anything before he drove the two-inch draining
needle into my back. He didn't say, for example, "Now it will
feel like a rabid wolverine ripping through your flesh to suck
out the life-juice." A warm sensation spread across my back
as fluid o'er-spilled the puncture. Dr. Tran showed me a test
tube full of light brown fluid. "It looks like this." He angled
the needle again and pushed it hard. Before long he had collected three litres of the stuff, which looked suspiciously like
beer. English bitter, of which I have had my share, and for a
second I thought that perhaps at some point, in my haste, I
had dumped a few pints down the wrong hole.

As painful as the ordeal was, every second it went on I felt
lighter, better. They left the bottles of fluid beside me for most
of the evening, and I spent the night in the emergency ward.
They asked if I wanted painkillers; although my back was
sore, I felt right enough. They asked if I wanted something to
help me sleep, but I thought I'd be able to manage it drug-free.
I was exhausted, spent. I still couldn't think of anyone to contact. I text-messaged a woman I'd known, briefly, the previous autumn. "I'm in the hospital."

"Yikes! What's wrong?"

"If I'm lucky," I punched out with my thumbs, "it's pneumonia."

I WAS discharged from the hospital, having had, as I say, more than three litres of fluid removed from the cavity surrounding my left lung. What I'd experienced was, to give it an impressive scientific name, a "massive pleural effusion." The high honcho doctor, head of Respirology, had come into my hospital room to tell me it was "obviously very serious," but he said it would take them a few days to figure out why, exactly, the fluid had accumulated. So home I went, supplied with some killer antibiotics, and in a few days I was feeling pretty good. Indeed, when my friend Shaughnessy called, checking up on me, I said, "You know what, Shaughn, I'm half-inclined to believe in God. Because, face it, I was kind of at a low point. I mean, there's no work..." (the Canadian television and movie industry, which is where I'd long made my pin money, was moribund, with nothing being produced) "... my career as a novelist isn't going anywhere..." (*The Ravine*, my last book, had been long-listed for the Giller Prize, but pretty much ignored after that) "... my personal life is a mess..." (which was, of course, more my fault than anybody else's) "... so maybe this health scare is God's way of saying, 'Hey, fatboy, you should appreciate what you've got.'"

And that was the attitude with which I, accompanied by Martin Worthy, my dear friend and a founding member of the musical group Porkbelly Futures, went to attend my consultation with Dr. Frazier on May 11, 2009.

"How are you feeling?" the doctor asked.

"I feel terrific," I said.

"Great, just great." Dr. Frazier picked up a file. "Well, we've got some answers for you. It's cancer. It's lung cancer—"

("Hold on, hold on!" I wanted to shout. "Didn't you just hear me tell you I felt terrific?")

"It's the non-small cell type of cancer. You have what we call a 'sessile' tumour. It's not what we'd call an operable cancer it's a you're a and think in terms of months andjkghghjgkkljhjkghjkghghjghjlshgjhkasjhkjashdjkn ..."

SO—WHERE DO we go from here? Well, like I said, I had just finished a little memoir about my life in music. That word, "memoir," suddenly acquired holy heft. The phrase "months to live" fires up all sorts of engines, most of them a little selfish (I've got to get laid a lot, I have to eat a forty-dollar Kobe beef hamburger), some of them a little more lofty. Namely, I wanted to write some of this down. So, I had this memoir, and my Publisher had asked for a rewrite, and he really liked the personal stuff, hmmm ...

"I'll need a couple of months with that second draft," I told the Publisher. "I'm just going to add a new thematic concern."

"Umm ... sure."

If I do my job well, this won't be quite the motley pastiche you might imagine. I've become very interested in the process of songwriting. Writing songs is a way to interact with the world, to take it in as experience (employment, job dismissals, hopeful first dates, clumsy hand-jobs, bad whisky, rejected marriage proposals, accepted marriage proposals, bad love, true love, long road trips, and pronouncements of fatal disease) and spit it out in three- to four-minute units of airborne beauty and grace. And at this point in my life—way closer to the end than I thought I'd be at the age of fifty-six—music has acquired more importance than it ever had.

When I was a small child, my favourite recording was something called "The Cigar Box Banjo." I summarized the story in *The Ravine*, but assuming you haven't read that novel—a reasonable assumption—I'm going to do so again here.

A boy makes a banjo out of a cigar box. (How, exactly, I didn't know at the time, and I won't detail here. These days, there are blueprints and schematics aplenty available at the click of a key. But it was a long-standing source of frustration for me as a kid that much of what excited me in the realm of fiction was impossible to duplicate in real life. I did get my hands on a cigar box, away back when, but that only made things worse, since I couldn't see how to attach a neck or strings.)

Anyway: this boy hears of a contest, a banjo-playing contest, taking place in the next town, some ten miles away. Despite the fact that the kid has nothing like a show piece, he decides he will go compete. So (without informing his parents, I remember, simply heading off) he begins to walk the dusty road. As he goes along, the lad hears things—a bluebird's song, for instance, the whine of truck tires, the lowing of a cow—and he imitates these things on his cigar box banjo, layering one upon another. By the time he reaches the contest site, he has an entire song. He plays this, and he wins.[3]

---

3 Ira Gershwin wrote in his diary: "Heard in a day: An elevator's purr, telephone's ring, telephone's buzz, a baby's moans, a shout of delight, a screech from a 'flat wheel,' hoarse honks, a hoarse voice, a tinkle, a match scratch on sandpaper, a deep resounding boom of dynamiting in the impending subway, iron hooks on the gutter."

I loved that story, and I think it stands as a reasonable template for the creative process.[4] As songwriters and novelists and musicians travel through their lives, they collect little themes and motifs and whistles and airs, and they string them together to fashion their wares. This book follows my travels down the musical road, and I intend to commence that forthwith.

---

4   I have one small quibble with the recording: the prize is a brand-new, store-bought banjo, which the kid happily accepts. I pictured him tossing away his jerry-rigged trash with disdain. This has always struck me as a poor choice, story-wise. It would have been much better if the kid had danced with the one that brought him, if you see what I mean—if he'd politely declined the grand prize.

CHAPTER

[1]

O N MY father's side of the family, everyone is either a teacher or a musician, except for those hopelessly indecisive sorts—my cousin Doug is an example—who have opted to become music teachers. My great-uncles, my grandfather's brothers, were all musicians, and that included Rance Quarrington, who was apparently a star of the radio waves, the possessor of wondrously mellow windpipes. (My brother Anthony B. Quarrington—Tony— claims that Rance starred in a movie entitled *The Man from Toronto,* but I have no evidence to support that. No evidence suggesting he *didn't* star in such a film, mind you.)

My grandfather himself had a long succession of careers. He was a travelling salesman for a while, back in the days when that vocation was conducted mostly by rail. He accumulated years and years of bumpy seat-time, and during this period he learned to walk a coin across his knuckles. As a child, I was greatly impressed with this little piece of legerdemain, constantly inveighing the elderly Jewish fellow who was my grandfather to walk a nickel or a quarter back and forth atop his fist. (No, I'm not Jewish, but I'm pretty sure my grandfather was. If you saw a photograph of Joe Quarrington, you would be convinced.) He was also a photographer, and set up shop as a portraitist. This was in the first quarter of the twentieth century, and those times being what they were—every bit as strange as these times—my grandfather attracted many customers who were interested in having their Kirlian auras captured on film. "Please take my portrait," they would say, "but not before I meditate for a few minutes." I imagine these people concentrating so hard that their faces coloured and steam shot out of their nostrils, but when my grandfather emerged later from the darkroom, there was never any evidence of Kirlian auras. I like to believe it was because he could not abide their disappointment that my grandfather took to dusting cornstarch onto the negatives before slipping them into the chemical bath. The resulting image showed the subject surrounded by a halo of feathery cloud, the air pregnant with luminous parhelions. Business picked up quite a bit.

I write of these things—the coin-knuckle thimbleriggery and the photographic flummery—because they both, to me, indicate personality traits common to musicians. Let's say, the willingness to invest thousands of hours toward a small, inconsequential end and the desire to please people. And indeed my grandfather could play many instruments and was a violinist in the no longer extant Ottawa Symphony.[1]

Tony, who is my older brother, acquired a banjo when we were kids. There was a folk revival going on, the movement that would spawn Bob Dylan. So Tony got a banjo, and the elderly Jewish fellow showed him how to play some chords. It was in this manner that live music entered our household. There were, to be sure, instruments in the house prior to this. An old, hulking piano resided in the basement. An African drum was spotted here and there, a small, exotic animal looking for a place to get comfortable. And there was an ocarina, too; my father would periodically pop the mouthpiece between his lips and wheeze out the theme from *The Third Man*.

Soon I wanted to play an instrument. (All this predates, by a few months, anyway, the advent of the Beatles, after which everybody and their brother decided to take up an instrument.) I started strumming along quite spiritedly on a mandolin, chosen because it was a small instrument and I owned a small hand. The first song I learned to play was a classic, "This Land Is Your Land." As first songs go, this was a pretty good one. There is wonderful power and poetry in the lyrics, and in adopting "This Land Is Your Land" as an ideal, a basic template, I had (unknowingly) set the bar rather high. I say "(unknowingly)" because I was preoccupied not only with fingering the chords but with trying to remember the words. It is a geographical song, and at least off the top is concerned with naming places. I have trouble retrieving mere lists from

1 Here's another bit of family lore I just learned from my brother Tony. Apparently, for a while, my grandfather played in a band that supplied entertainment on some sort of pleasure vessel, a huge paddleboat or something, that cruised down the Don River. That's a lovely bit of family lore, but I'm not going to fact-check it too aggressively, if you see what I mean. If you could see and smell the Don River these days, you would share some of my misgivings. But the story goes that Joe Quarrington played in the band, and also featured on board—her act consisting of "Recitation and Elocution"— was Nora Fleischer, who was to become my grandmother. Tony says he has seen the playbill, even thinks that he possesses a copy of it, but Tony is a pathological collector, and the chances of finding any one thing in his collections is remote.

the memory banks. Moreover, there was a Canadian version ("from Bonavista to Vancouver Island"), and I was torn between this version and the "real" one, so often I bellowed out an odd combination of the two.[2]

WOODROW WILSON Guthrie was born in Okemah, Oklahoma, in 1912, the son of a businessman, landowner, and Democratic politician. (I mean, his father was all those things; it wasn't my intention to suggest some Satanic trinity.) Woodrow was a bright lad, and he read constantly. That didn't prevent him from leaving high school before graduation. It is said he picked up harmonica by hanging around a street corner beside a black man and his shoeshine box. He learned a little guitar in order to accompany his cousin, a fiddler. And that's what Woody was, a widely read kid who could play a little music, when he joined the thousands of Okies travelling westward to California, where, it was said, there was work. This was the Dust Bowl era, and out on the coast was the mythical "pie in the sky."[3]

I don't know at what point Guthrie became "politicized," a word I've put in quotes mostly because it makes me kind of uneasy. I sometimes conflate Woody Guthrie and John Steinbeck's fictional Tom Joad. In *The Grapes of Wrath*, Joad is made increasingly aware of injustice and suffering; he discovers the worth of every single human being, regardless of wealth or origin, and he goes out into the world to fight for the dignity

---

2   There is also, I've since learned, an Irish version of this song ("from the hills of Kerry to the streets of Derry"), a Scottish version, a Swedish version, an Israeli version ("from the Negev Desert to the heights of Golan"), and so forth.

3   That phrase, "pie in the sky," was coined by Joe Hill in his song "The Preacher and the Slave." Hill, another honorary godfather of the folkie protest song, was executed for a murder he didn't commit.

of all. I believe something like that happened to Guthrie; indeed, one of his most enduring songs is "Tom Joad." Guthrie was also inspired to write a song about Thomas Mooney, a labour leader imprisoned for bombing the Preparedness Day march of 1916 (killing ten and injuring forty), a crime virtually no one thought he actually committed. But as the fine songwriter Steve Earle once remarked, "I don't think of Woody Guthrie as a political writer. He was a writer who lived in very political times." I'm guessing that Guthrie was inspired by a good story as much as by his outrage. After all, he did write "Pretty Boy Floyd." The song makes an eloquent point about the callousness of banks ("some rob with a fountain pen"), but Charles Arthur Floyd was pretty much a murdering thug.

Guthrie's songs soon found an audience, and he began singing "hillbilly" music on radio station KFVD. There he met newscaster Ed Robbin, a left-leaning fellow who introduced Guthrie to socialists and Communists in Southern California, including a man who would become Woody's lifelong friend, Will Geer.[4] Many of you will remember Geer as Zebulon (Grandpa) Walton, but it is interesting to note that Geer was also a folksinger and a political radical. "Which means I get to the root of things," Geer was fond of saying. "That's the Latin derivation for 'radical.'" Geer refused to testify before the House Committee on Un-American Activities and was subsequently blacklisted. His solution was to start a theatre company called Theatricum Botanicum, in which he and other blacklisted players presented the works of the Bard.

---

4   Although Guthrie wrote 174 "Woody Sez" columns for *The Daily Worker*, he was never an actual Communist Party member. I don't know why I bothered to include that as a footnote; I think it's just a knee-jerk reaction for a kid of the fifties to note whether an individual was, or had ever been, a member of the Communist Party.

Geer, busy on the Broadway stage, invited Guthrie to New York City. It was there Woody made his first real recordings, musicologist Alan Lomax feeling that Guthrie's songs should be documented for the Library of Congress.[5] Guthrie decided to respond to the over-popularity of Kate Smith's "God Bless America." He had seen too much to endorse that kind of cheery chauvinism. He borrowed a melody from an old gospel song, "Oh My Loving Brother." Although he wrote about the physical grandeur of America in "This Land Is Your Land," he got a few good digs in too. Not everyone knows the final two verses to the song, in which Guthrie sees hungry people lined up outside a relief office and wonders if this land is really made for you and me.

Song can be an effective vehicle for political statement, in particular for complaint and damnation, song being an extension of speech, and speech being what it is. Alan Lomax described a scene that occurred during the "ballad hunting" he undertook with his father across the American South.

> A few ragged sharecroppers had been gathered together by the plantation manager to sing for us. They had sung some spirituals, and finally everybody said, "Let's have Old Blue sing." A big Black man stood up in front of the tiny Edison cylinder recorder. He said, "I want to sing my song right into it—I don't want to sing it in advance." We said, "Well, we

5 Lomax was the son of pioneering musicologist John Lomax, and had travelled widely with his father recording authentic folk music. At the Angola Prison Farm, the Lomaxes encountered a man who was physically intimidating and immensely popular with his fellow inmates for the songs he sang. They recorded hours of this fellow, then sent the warden a request for clemency, including a recording of this fellow's most popular song, "Good Night, Irene." Huddie Ledbetter—Leadbelly, as he was better known—was pardoned.

would like to hear it first because we don't have very many unused cylinders." He said, "No sir, you are going to have to have this right straight from the beginning." We agreed, and so he sang:

> Work all week
> Don't make enough
> To pay my board
> And buy my snuff.
> It's hard, it's hard
> It's hard on we poor farmers,
> It's hard.

After a few more stanzas, he spoke into the recorder horn as though it was a telephone. He said, "Now, Mr. President, you just don't know how bad they're treating us folks down here. I'm singing to you and I'm talking to you so I hope you will come down here and do something for us poor folks here in Texas."

On another afternoon in the early twentieth century, on a street corner in Spokane, Washington, a political agitator named Jack Walsh was busily recruiting for the Industrial Workers of the World, standing on a soapbox and preaching unionism. Down the road, the Salvation Army was recruiting on its own behalf. The Holy Soldiers disliked Walsh's exhortations of revolution, so they elected to march the band down—tambourines pounding, trombones baying, trumpets keening—and attempt to drown him out. Walsh fought back, starting a musical aggregation of his own that included Harry "Haywire Mac" McClintock pounding out cadence on a bass drum. Among the songs McClintock wrote was "Big Rock Candy Mountain," a beautiful evocation of a hobo's Utopia. McClintock had another song, "Hallelujah, I'm a Bum," which the street-corner crowds found very rousing. Walsh penned a couple of parodies of the Sally Ann's high-test spirituals, "When the Roll Is Called Up Yonder" and "Where Is My Wandering Boy Tonight?" Those four songs became the foundation of the IWW's *Little Red Songbook*, which sold for ten cents. The volume soon contained not only more songs but "The Preamble," the manifesto of the Industrial Workers of the World:

> The working class and the employing class have nothing in common. There can be no peace so long as hunger and want are found among millions of working people and the few, who make up the employing class, have all the good things in life.

It's hard to say how this all connects to a chubby little eleven-year-old kid playing "This Land Is Your Land" with cross-eyed, tongue-biting concentration. I knew nothing then of pie in the sky or sharecroppers or the Industrial Workers of the World. All I knew was that Woody Guthrie's song was fun to play and sing. Without realizing it, I suspect I was also absorbing the idea that songs should *mean* something, that they should make a point, and that the point should be beneficial.

I had another musical lesson coming, too. At the end of seven months of arduous performance on the mandolin on my part, my younger brother, Joel, came along, picked up the mandolin, stared at it for a few seconds, and then proceeded to play it with aplomb. Tony, meanwhile, had become something of a hotshot on the banjo. Suddenly there was a guitar in the house as well, and Tony began his adventures on the fretboard, adventures that continue to this day. All of which is to say, my brothers very quickly demonstrated themselves to be much more musically gifted than I.

I could, however, sing. When I sang, pleasant things happened. My father would pause in the doorway to his den and pull on his pipe reflectively. My mother would lay aside her book (for she read constantly), and a vague, somewhat wistful smile would visit. When we three brothers joined forces, my brothers would let me sing lead, while Joel undertook the higher harmony and Tony essayed the bass.

The music we favoured was bluegrass, popularized in those days by groups like the New Lost City Ramblers. During those sessions with my brothers, I imprinted upon myself particular notions of music-making. For one thing, in bluegrass (the result of a backwoods tryst between English traditional folk music and the blues), instrumental virtuosity is encouraged, the musicians bellying forward in turn to improvise over the changes. Also, bluegrass features harmonies, dense and often a little dissonant, the characteristic "high lonesome" wail of Bill Monroe. And I adopted, back then, an iconography of trains and birds and churches that would show up later in my songs. Finally, bluegrass music, for all its up-tempo spirit, often embraces dark subject matter: murder, alcoholism, the untimely death of loved ones.

ALL RIGHT: on that note, here comes the new thematic material. As Martin and I drove home from the meeting with Dr. Frazier, we weren't sure how to proceed. There seemed to be very little to do. Very little to say. At one point Martin ventured, "Well, I guess if you ever wondered what you'd do if someone gave you that news, now you know."

"Uh-huh."

Martin is not technically my oldest friend, but he is my dearest. He had come with me to the doctor because several people had suggested it was good to have two sets of ears. But the truth of the matter was, Marty had been every bit as gobsmacked as I, and neither of us had heard much more than dick-all of what was said. Somewhere in there Dr. Frazier had seemed to suggest that I was going to die in a few months.

I called Dorothy at work. Dorothy and I had divorced several years prior to all this, but when I first got ill she took me back into the house on First Avenue. (The house on First Avenue is next door to the house owned by Martin and his wife, Jill, which is no coincidence. We bought the houses together, two adjacent row houses, and then we tore down the fence separating the gardens, giving us a larger shared space. This wasn't done for any *Bob & Carol & Ted & Alice* type reasons, rather so that both couples would have handy babysitting. Indeed, my daughters, Carson and Flannery, think of Marty and Jill as a second set of parents, especially since their first set of parents split up.)

Anyway, Dorothy worked part time for E & C Marine, the "C" of which was Charles Gallimore, who had sold me my houseboat, and she arrived home a little while later, seeming very calm and collected. (I found out later, from Charles, that she'd done her crying there in the shop, a nor'easter of misery, so that she could appear at home unruffled and strong.) "So, it's lung cancer?" she asked.

"Uh-huh."

Again. Very little to do. Very little to say. We exchanged

words of some sort, and then I announced, "Well, I think I'll go for a little drive."

I headed, without thinking, toward the east, way out into Scarborough. As I drove, I said, under my breath, "Fuck fuck fuck fuck" over and over again.

My cell phone rang. It was Shaughnessy, who often phones up to see how I am. I dare say he didn't expect such a blunt answer: "I've got lung cancer."

"What?"

"Non-operable."

"Shit shit shit shit."

"No, it's fuck fuck fuck fuck." I tried to be stoic, saying as how I had led a good life, and had lovely friends and loved ones. But then the sight of a very pretty girl reduced me to convulsive sobs. "I'm going to miss this so much," I managed to get out, although my throat was so knotted with remorse that speech seemed hardly possible. I told Shaughn that I'd call him back later, and I drove on down to the Bluffs.

Some brief earth-science history: over many millennia, the eastern end of the land that modern Toronto sits upon eroded, and the effluvia ribboned across the water to the west. Over time, it formed a long, bent peninsula; a storm in the nineteenth century severed and separated this landmass, which now forms the Toronto Islands. The Bluffs are fascinating, to me, on several counts. For one thing, they are beautiful, in a bleak and desolate way. They rise hundreds of feet into the air, with the kind of naked nature, lifeless and alien, that one encounters in hoodoos and mesas.

The Bluffs are also associated in my mind with death. I don't believe this was at the forefront of my mind as I drove there on D-Day, Diagnosis Day. But throughout my childhood

I heard stories of people meeting their end on the Bluffs, either by suicide or when a part of the cliffside suddenly collapsed. A very popular art teacher at my high school lived on the Bluffs; his young daughter was standing close to the edge one day when the earth disappeared from beneath her feet, and she was gone. So maybe this was leading me down to the Bluffs, on some level: it seemed a place to go to begin battle with the Darkness. ("To begin negotiations" might be more accurate.)

Various species of birds inhabit the Scarborough Bluffs, evolution having brought them to this particular place of endless bickering and squawking. Any scrap of food is the epicentre of a convergence of ungodly screech and ululation. Wings are beaten menacingly, necks ruffled. The only relatively quiet species is the swan. Those elegant creatures maintain their silence, for the same reason the crazed and homicidal do: to keep their victims unsuspecting and unprepared. I mention this because, having driven down the huge hill and left the car in the lot, I stumbled out to the shore and bawled like a baby. Not non-stop. But every minute or so I would emit a long wail of, oh, who knows what the emotion was at that point? The truest thing to say would be that it wasn't a single emotion, it was quite a few of them stumbling into each other to get out, like drunkards in a doorway.

In the midst of all this, a swan snuck up behind me and bit me on the ass.

I was of course very indignant, but the creature had a point. Get on with it. I started back toward my car. My first resolution: no more cheap wine. I drove back to First Avenue, stopping at the LCBO on the way to buy some Borolos and Amarones.

We held an impromptu wake.

CHAPTER

[**2**]

I HAVE ONLY a handful of vivid childhood memories, and here's one of them: I was on a sleepover at my friend Kenny's house. I was in the top bunk normally occupied by his brother, because his brother was out somewhere, and we were watching television late at night, because, well, I became a television addict early on in life, and Kenny was more addicted than I. We had managed to pull in an American signal—not always possible in those days of rabbit ears—and were watching *The Jack Paar Show*. I don't suppose the show interested us much, for the most part, but it was American and therefore superior to anything the Canadian Broadcasting Corporation might put on the airwaves.

Jack Paar said something about something being a sensation in Britain, and our ears perked up. The television screen filled with the image of four young men, similarly suited. All four men sported "Buster Brown" haircuts, a term I use because that is what I read subsequently, somewhere in the thousands of pages of Beatles-related material I ingested. I associated that particular hairstyle with Moe Howard, the nasty, eye-poking leader of the Three Stooges.

That TV event heralded a trip we all went on back then, one that took us to England, and to India, and to recesses of our minds no doubt better left untouched. Not a lot of that is germane here. The important thing to note is, we all started forming *groups*.

I don't suppose I'd be a songwriter today if it hadn't been for Paul McCartney and John Lennon. Their songs appeared in my life one by one—each wondrous, almost miraculous, each announcing itself boldly as a Lennon/McCartney composition. Lennon/McCartney, as an entity, seemed to be the most creative force ever unleashed upon the face of the earth. Of course, we eventually learned that Lennon/McCartney didn't really exist, that it was a label of convenience. If John wrote a song, he credited it as Lennon/McCartney. Paul did likewise. I recently heard a rumour that Sir Paul is trying to change the order of the names, to alter the designation legally to McCartney/Lennon. It might seem a bit small-minded, but I say, hey, he's the living one, he's survived hellish marriages and kept playing music, so he should get the credit he deserves.

I must admit I don't have much to say about individual Lennon/McCartney songs. I enjoy "You've Got to Hide Your Love Away," and often introduce it into impromptu sing-alongs, but that's largely so that I can shout "Hey!" at (or around) the appropriate time. (I think this also reflects my attraction to the point of view adopted by Lennon in the song, the stance of surly self-centredness.) "Here, There and Everywhere" is a very beautiful song, and it has what we might call "sophisticated chord changes," which means that as teenagers we were baffled and unable to work them out. There is, if you'll allow me to get technical, a modulation to the bridge in that song, and at those same singalongs, you might notice that with the words "I want her everywhere," the bottom usually drops out of the accompaniment bag, leaving the singers crooning eerily on their own.

The assertion that pop music, rock'n'roll, is informed by a mere three chords is a myth propagated largely by non-musicians. The statement correctly points to a simplicity, an eloquence, in some of the music, but there are surprisingly few songs that the young, aspiring guitarist can actually execute with just three chords.[1] "Summertime Blues," that'll work. That's actually a song wherein knowing more than three chords might prove a detriment. And Van Morrison's classic "Gloria" can be played with three chords, but they aren't the usual three chords. Rock'n'roll's three chords are the tonic, the sub-dominant, and the dominant. The sixteen-year-old Morrison was thrashing away at the tonic, the flattened seven, and the sub-dominant. "Gloria" also contains a little guitar fill that seems to follow these changes with a logic born on the fretboard. In reality, there is a fingering change that must be made. As teenagers we usually pretended that wasn't the case, and many of us still do, just in case you're wondering why that instrumental part always sounds like crap when your buddy

---

[1] Part of the problem is that designation rock'n'roll, which I feel stupid even typing, seeing as I had to use two apostrophes. I suppose if we accept the term as referring to a very restricted sub-segment of popular music, the three-chord assertion makes sense. Actually, three chords might represent the upper limit. "Bo Diddley," for example, is a one-chord song, or one and a partial, although I myself play two full chords. But when we were thirteen years old and figuring out chords, it wasn't to play "pop" music—we applied the term "rock'n'roll" to everything. I guess we would have averred, without blinking, that Mrs. Miller singing "A Lover's Concerto" was rock'n'roll.

plays it. As a young lad, I spent thousands and thousands of hours trying to work out changes—to "figure out the chords"—so believe me about this three-chord business. Even a seemingly simplistic ballad from the fifties—"You Send Me," for example—has *four* chords.

Paul McCartney's "Yesterday" was a Gordian knot, an impenetrable puzzle. I sat in my bedroom for days on end trying to work it out, intuiting that the ability to play and sing "Yesterday" would increase my chances of getting laid. (Or getting kissed, or fondling a breast, or even remaining in reasonably close proximity to a female human being for more than a few seconds.) There are chords, as you may know, made by stopping some strings and leaving others free to vibrate. These have the pleasing name of "open chords." Other chords—"bar chords," we call them, although "closed chords" conveys the right impression—require that all the strings be dampened, usually by a flattened index finger. This is not the easiest skill to acquire, in terms of either dexterity or strength, because it's hard to slam all six strings down with a single finger and still have them sound boldly. "A" is a great key, because most of the important chords (the fourth, the fifth, even the "Gloria" flattened seven) are open chords. It's a great key on the guitar, that is; saxophonists don't care for it. If the guitar player is playing in A, then a tenor saxophonist has to transpose (the instrument actually sounds a tone lower than the written note) to the key of B, which has five sharps. Five sharps represent a lot of cowflaps in the musical pasture, if you see what I mean. It is for this reason that the sax player is *always* the best musician in the band.

But, getting back to "Yesterday." The first chord on the recording is an F, a bar chord. Some people play F in a manner necessitating that the index finger be bent at the first joint, that the thumb wrap around and stop the low bass string. As complicated as that sounds, it's often preferable to trying to pull off the infernally difficult F bar chord.[2]

Despite all this whining on my part, "Yesterday" is the most recorded song ever. There are something like three thousand covers. One way of explaining this is that while the song may lack "guitar logic," it makes a lot of musical sense.[3] Indeed, it makes so much musical sense that apparently Paul McCartney was initially unsure that he had truly composed the music. He was afraid he had inadvertently pilfered some standard.

BEFORE WE continue with our story, here's a little aside. You're probably wondering, if he's stopping the proceedings to make an aside, then what are all those footnotes about? Well, you don't have to read the footnotes if you don't want to, but you should pay attention to these asides. I might be introducing characters, new players in the scenario, which is the case here.

Michael Burke was a fellow I met around this time—when I was thirteen, I believe—as he attended the same junior high school I did. He was a heavy-set boy with a big, bushy beard. Well, I suppose it's improbable that he had the beard at fourteen, but he grew it at the first available opportunity and has owned it ever since. These days, that beard is somewhat out

2 Some people don't bother to stop that low string with their thumb, either, the idea being that they will thence avoid smacking the open, dissonant low E string. They rarely do.

3 There are some songs that abound in "guitar logic." The introduction to "Knock on Wood," for example, is a power-chord ascension up the guitar fretboard. It was written by Steve Cropper, who then reversed things and came back down for the introduction to "Midnight Hour."

of hand. It ambles off his face and rests on his sweatshirt, which is an essential component of Michael's preferred wardrobe. Burke—I usually refer to him as "Burkie" or "Mickie" or "Burkle," as in "Mickle Burkle"—has often averred that he chose his course in life so that he could avoid jackets and neckties. His course in life revolved around computers. When we were boys, he took Computer Science very seriously. In those days, the subject involved punch cards and farm machinery. Burkie and another lad, Rob Dunn, lacking sufficient access to the actual mechanical works, would take turns writing programs (punching out chads on those damnable yellow cards) and then passing the stack of cards to the other, who would act as the computer and execute. Fairly geeky behaviour, it's true, but both boys went on to find great fortune in the burgeoning field of personal computing. Some years ago, Burkie started a company that, as he puts it, "decided to concentrate its efforts on a little-known thing called the Internet." Specifically, the company made and distributed firewalls. All of which is to say, Burkie soon had money, lots of it. He sold the company to become an arts entrepreneur; he started a record company. (This reminds me of the stories you hear about people who receive a huge amount of money through inheritance or some other windfall, and are then driven by guilt to throw or fritter it away.)

Mike Burke owns the company that released our second CD, *Porkbelly Futures*, so he will figure in this story in various ways. But for our current purposes, his significance is this. Mickle's fortune has allowed him to indulge his long-lived passion for the Beatles. He has, in a lovely house in Victoria, British Columbia, a room devoted to record albums, reel-to-reel tapes, all manner of recorded rarities created by the Fab

Four. I happened to be visiting not so long ago when Michael played me the most interesting thing, a recording of Paul McCartney teaching the other Beatles the chords to his new song, "Yesterday."

"F major," we hear Paul saying. "E minor, A seventh, D minor—" McCartney leaves off his rhythmic intoning momentarily to instruct, "Don't watch my hand. The guitar's tuned down, so I'm playing in G."

The importance of this may well be lost on you, but me, I was stunned. I had spent much of my life grumbling about the fucking F chord that begins the song, and all this time McCartney wasn't even playing one. He'd cunningly tuned his guitar down a whole tone, so that he could strum a Cowboy G. And that little term, "Cowboy G," deserves a footnote.[4]

WELL, THEN, the Beatles arrived, and we started forming groups.

My brother Joel and I immediately came up with plans that involved a) pop music and b) total global domination of the sort demonstrated by the Liverpudlians. (Tony was never really attacked by the British Invasion. He seemed to know the chords to all the Beatles songs, but he persisted in his folksy ways, forming a bluegrass band called the Gangrene Boys. He hung around Toronto's Yorkville area, the Village, and was sitting around someone's kitchen table one day, drinking wine and smoking grass, etcetera, when Neil Young

---

4 Guitar chords in their most simplistic fingerings are often given the appellation "cowboy." A Cowboy G, for example, created with three fingers (there's also a better sounding formation that requires four), allows the B string to sound boldly. Because it's impossible to tune a B string precisely—and I don't mean difficult, I mean impossible—the chord sounds in a rowdy manner, the fanfare for a plaintive yodel.

rushed in and announced that he was driving to California. "Anyone want to come?" Tony had academic ambitions in those days—he was assiduously studying Ezra Pound's *Cantos* at the university—so he declined. There is a dent in his butt where he's been kicking himself all these years since.) Anyway, Joel and I started a group. The instrumentation was somewhat fluid. We both hammered away on guitars, and sometimes I pounded on the piano. There was even a snare drum/cymbal combination that I'd received as a Christmas present, which seems to indicate that maybe my parents were hitting the liquor cabinet a little heavily that particular holiday season. But we needed more people for our group, which I had decided should be called PQ's People.

Now, I understand that groups had existed before the British Invasion. Indeed, because of my brother Tony and his folkie ways, I was acquainted with all sorts of groups. The New Lost City Ramblers, as I've mentioned. The Kingston Trio. Bluegrass music was nothing *but* groups; there's really no such thing as a bluegrass solo artist, and Bill Monroe had his Blue Grass Boys. But, perhaps because there was such a massive tsunami of publicity material, the Beatles impressed upon us that a group was made of distinct and disparate components, with the whole being much greater than the sum of its parts. There was quiet, introspective George, rebellious John, romantic Paul, and, um, whatever Ringo was. The implication was that none of these guys could survive on his own, that their individualism would otherwise not allow them to function in society. That concept appealed to those of us who felt *we* couldn't function in society. When I was a lad, that included everyone except Vance Milligan and a couple of girls in grade eleven. So, in assembling a group, Joel and I had extra-musical considerations. It was all right that we were brothers—the Kinks had brothers, Ray and Dave Davies— and better than all right, since Joel was red- and curly-haired, and my hair was dark and straight. But we needed to be complemented by other distinct types.

My father had a colleague, Dr. Hill, and occasionally these two men would encounter one another, at the grocery or liquor store, or simply strolling along the sidewalk. Dr. Hill was a large man, tall and burly, as was my father. Sometimes both men had offspring with them. Joel and I would hide behind our dad and take suspicious peeks at the two kids who were hiding behind *their* dad. The older one was named Danny, the younger, Larry. When Joel and I formed PQ's People, we remembered that Danny had some musical ability, that he was taking guitar lessons and had been heard to sing songs. So we auditioned him. We held the audition down in our basement one day when our fathers were upstairs drinking beer and being colleagues. We were all pretty short back then, and Danny climbed up on a table, employing it as a makeshift stage. He used a drumstick as a microphone—no, it didn't work—and such was his eagerness to perform that he didn't wait for Joel and me to pick up our instruments. Not that we knew the tune he sang, anyway, which was, I seem to recall, Sinatra's "Summer Wind." Danny crooned in a very Las Vegas fashion. He even had a repertoire of cheesy moves, which he threw at us without self-consciousness or irony. My brother and I didn't know what to make of it. Danny would have been a good addition to PQ's People; he was a good-looking kid and exotic to us, being as his mother was white and Dr. Hill black. But his style didn't seem right, so we thanked him for his time and told him we'd be in touch.

WE CONTINUED searching for candidates, minuscule musicians willing to join PQ's People. (By the way, Joel went on record early on, declaring the band name to be stupid. But I was his older, bigger brother, and while I certainly didn't win every fight, I was willing to go to the mat on this one. So PQ's People we remained.) We encountered a young lad named Conrad, and he had the most wondrous of all things, a set of drums. At least, he had access to a set of drums, as his stepfather was a drummer.

Conrad lived in the maisonettes a few blocks away. (Where I come from, the nascent suburbs of Toronto, Ontario, we didn't really measure distances in "blocks." We tended to mark destinations by what lay in the way: a street, a school, the ominous ravine.) Down in the basement of his townhouse was a music room. Can you believe that, a music room? It contained not just a set of drums, which sat in the centre of the room with proprietorial majesty, but the makings of several more sets. Tom-toms, snares, and kick drums were strewn about everywhere. Gleaming golden cymbals leaned against the wall. There were strange percussion instruments as well, African gourds, djembes, and congas. Joel and I would haul our equipment over there, and Conrad would climb aboard the stool behind the kit, and we would play "Satisfaction." I will try to help you imagine the sound, because the Rolling Stones version is no doubt playing in your mind, and that is not the same as the rendition performed by PQ's People. The cheapness of our amps and guitars is germane. Joel and I had both blown the paper cones of our speakers, so along with the music came much chittering distortion. My guitar was a Zenon, a solid body with very hard action. I don't mean to keep getting technical on you, but "action" refers to the ease with which strings can be clamped down onto the fretboard. It required much concentration to wrestle with the Zenon's strings, so the famous "Satisfaction" riff stumbled out as though it were wearing clumpy leg braces.[5]

Now, what I've been withholding from you is that Conrad's stepfather wasn't simply a drummer. He was Ed Thigpen, whose musical career included stints with people like Ella Fitzgerald, Duke Ellington, and, most famously, Canada's own Oscar Peterson. Ed Thigpen was a bona fide jazz legend. Mind you, the term "jazz legend" didn't signify much to me back then, and it's only now, in adulthood, that I realize what an honour it was to make his acquaintance.

Which I did in the following manner. Imagine the lads down in the music room, gritting their way through "Satisfaction." We performed it with grim sobriety, our entire beings occupied with technical matters: the riff, the structure of the song (recall that at one point, everything falls away except the drums; leastwise, that's the plan), the lyrics. Ed Thigpen entered, listened as we arrived clumsily at the musical finish line, and then waved Conrad off the stool. "Let me play with these boys," he said.

Okay. Conrad hopped down, Mr. Thigpen took his position, and Joel and I began the riff. Ed—I guess I can call him Ed; after all, we were jamming, weren't we?—allowed us to

---

5 B–B–B–C#–D, when playing in the key of E. And there's no other key you can play it in. I mean, of course there are other keys, eleven if my sketchy music theory suffices. But this is another instance of guitar logic, something that makes illuminating sense given the mechanics of the instrument. The last note is usually played upon an open string, allowing even a struggling twelve-year-old guitarist the opportunity to finger the accompanying chord—which is impossible to do without executing the swaggering pelvic twitch that possesses Keith Richards when he plays this little riff, his most famous composition.

execute the lick once as establishment, and then he began to play along.

Well, I never. My initial thought, I'll confess, was that Conrad's stepdad was lying about being a professional drummer, because he appeared to be, well, spazzing out, waving his arms in broad circular motions, the sticks just happening to deflect off cowhide and metal. Drummers were supposed to move with robotic precision, and if they wanted to hit a cymbal, it seemed to me, they should turn and look at the thing for a full two seconds, addressing it, making sure it hadn't moved away somehow, before whacking it. Ed's eyes were elsewhere, and while I don't suppose they actually rolled up into the inside of his skull, that is certainly the impression I received. But soon I became aware that there was a presence in the room, a force with the power of a tidal wave. At least, it was far, far stronger than my twiddling little Keith Richards lick.

This was rhythm.

I had never encountered rhythm at close quarters before, certainly had never been trapped with it in a basement, where it bullied me up against the wall and slapped me around. "This Land Is Your Land" does not prepare a fellow for rhythm. Oh, certainly, that song has rhythm, but it has rhythm like an old woman might have a poodle, a dog with clipped fur and papers that give its legal name as "Lancelot of Les Halles." This rhythm was like an atavistic mastiff, only a mutated gene away from ferity.

It was scary.

Joel seemed to be battling rhythm more valiantly than I. He was playing with exhilaration, and a broad grin had blossomed across his freckled face. Indeed, if rhythm were a bucking bronco, he did his eight seconds. But you're right, I should dispense with metaphors, not only because I keep mixing 'em up, but because they are weak and unnecessary. Rhythm is elemental, something we have inside us like bile and marrow. The *access* can be a little problematic, since it is protected by self-consciousness and notions of seemliness. Let me put it this way. The fear I felt as Ed Thigpen played the drums was not *like* the fear I felt when I considered asking Mathilda to dance—it was *exactly the same fear*.

I'M TALKING about the fear of giving oneself over, I guess, of abandonment to the unknown, surrender to the moment. I suppose that's the connection back to my new thematic material. I'm not referring simply to the fear of death—we will talk about that in the pages to come, I'll warrant—but the fear of losing control. Especially since everyone wants to wrest control away from you. The people who love you want to take care of you, which makes sense. In their eyes, you may be demonstrating an inability to take care of yourself. People also have much advice: how to spend the few months left to you, how to best deal with this thing they call "cancer." People come to visit, which is great, except that sometimes you need to be doing other things. I wanted to write; I had this second draft to complete and a television show to develop. I had songs to write and record. I probably wouldn't have time to write another novel, but I thought a novella might be a possibility, perhaps just a long short story. But people had all sorts of notions of things I could and *should* be doing. Visiting Ireland, for example. My friend Jake communicated an offer from my fishing buddies, those lads with whom I make an annual journey to the bonefishing grounds that surround Cuba. "Anywhere in the world you want to go," said Jake, "we'll take you there."

"The truth of the matter is, Mako," I told him, "if I were to die tomorrow, it wouldn't be one of my big regrets, that I didn't fish enough." That fact is entirely due to Jake, who dreams big and then connives ways to make things happen. We have gone many places in the world, on assignment, our adventures paid for by the editors of various magazines, often the generous (and fishing-obsessed) Pat Walsh, editor of *Outdoor Canada*. Jake and I call each other "Mako" and "Thresher," both appellations being species of shark. If that seems hopelessly ten years old to you, well, it kind of is. When I'm with the boys, I'm ten years old. When I'm with a woman, I mature slightly, and I mean ever so slightly, to fourteen or fifteen, giddy and hormone-addled, unable to believe that I am actually *with a woman*. Anyway, I said to Jake, "If I were to die tomorrow, it wouldn't be one of my big regrets, that I didn't fish enough. So I'm thinking maybe... Paris?"

But you lose most control, I think, to the doctors. A couple of days after my diagnosis, I went to meet the team who would be looking after me. That's how Toronto East General Hospital works. There was a team of doctors, consisting of Dr. Li (the chemo doctor), Dr. —— (radiation), and Dr. Simone (the thoracic surgeon). Of them all, I liked Dr. Simone—Carmine Simone—the best. He was a dark-haired young man, a touch on the burly side, who shook my hand and greeted me warmly as "the guest of honour." Dr. Li was quite an attractive young woman, so you might think I would have liked *her* the best, but she was a bit reserved. She spoke using statistics, and you know what Mark Twain said about statistics. For example, one of the first things she said was that the median life expectancy for someone with my condition was one year.

It took a while, a few weeks even, for me to realize what this meant. Not the "you're going to die" part. I got that. But the mathematical meaning—that half of the people with stage iv lung cancer live less than a year, half of them more than a year, with no cap or restriction on the time thereafter— was long in coming.

Dr. ——, the radiation guy, dismissed himself from our meeting early on. In a friendly enough way, he said that I was not a candidate for radiation, unless they were to discover that the cancer had already spread to my brain, in which case they would radiate before they did any chemo. The plan was to hit me with first-line chemicals, the ones that were most successful in most cases.

"But," Dr. Li said, "the statistics show that this chemotherapy on average extends life expectancy by only two or three months."

"Okay," we asked. Dorothy, Martin, and Jill were with me. "What does that mean?"

"It means that if two people both have your condition, and one receives chemotherapy and one doesn't, the first will outlive the other, probably, by two to three months."

"Oh," said I.

Still, I was more than willing to undergo chemotherapy, because, well, I was scared, and it seemed time to fight like a puma with its ass backed up against a wall. "Besides," I announced, "what's the use of being a big burly boy if you can't take a little chemo?" I have always bounced back and forth between "stocky" and, well, "fat," but all of a sudden this was a good thing. The chemo might very well have a negative effect on my appetite (*let's see it try,* said I), and I would lose weight, so it was good, Dr. Li observed, that I had something in reserve. My friend (and the Porkbelly keyboardist) Richard Bell died of cancer, and before he did he lost an appalling percentage of himself from the therapy. True, Richard recovered enough to play on our second album, but then he died. It seemed somehow to me that he had simply vanished into thin air.

The first couple of weeks following a dire diagnosis are pure and utter chaos, and chemotherapy seemed like the best path to follow. Indeed, the doctors took me on a tour of the chemo centre at the hospital, and it was a strangely upbeat place. People sat in comfy chairs, attached to the apparatus that delivered the chemicals, and read books or played board games with their visitors. The woman in charge said that in a recent survey, the chemotherapy ward had received a 100 per cent patient satisfaction rating. That's pretty impressive for a place where people are getting various poisons pumped into their bodies in order to destroy wild, rampaging C cells. We were introduced to a man named Wilson, who, when he was admitted to hospital, had been emaciated and spitting up blood. (See, if I'd been emaciated and spitting up blood, I might not have been quite so dim-witted with my self-diagnosis.) Wilson was on his last round of chemo (he had stage IV lung cancer, like me, so he got six doses, spaced three weeks apart, also my designated course), and he looked great. He was bright-eyed and smiling, and he'd actually put on weight!

But then something happened. Not long after D-Day, I went to interview Joe Hall, in whose musical ensemble, the Continental Drift, I had played throughout much of my twenties. In those years, Joe was typically wild-eyed, and he trailed liquor and pharmaceutical effluvia in his wake. But for the past many years, he has been sober and living in Peterborough, Ontario, where he's raised a couple of new kids and written some wonderful songs. The local arts community had decided to honour Joe, and I was asked to interview him onstage as part of the process.

Joe was always lean, but maturity has rendered him gaunt, his face a chiaroscuro, light beaming from his eyes, shadow in the shallow of his cheeks. He was very excited about this celebration of his life, which he referred to as Putting Joe out to Pasture Day. Many local musicians were on hand, and all of the former Continental Drifters were there. Indeed, George Dobo, the original keyboardist, and his wife had been living for several months in the house directly beside Joe's.

I would like to transcribe some of the interview for you, but in order to do so I would have to revisit the taped version, because I have very little memory of what took place. It is not so much that I was drunk or anything; the problem was that I was in some discomfort and labouring for breath. I didn't like the sight of even small flights of stairs; five or six risers, and I was huffing and puffing. Being me, of course, I put this down to a hangover—or, at least, I was unable to distinguish hangover pain from cancer-related pain. But here's a brief exchange:

JOE: I remember sitting in the Dominion Hotel in Vancouver, and I said to you, "We need drugs." And *you* responded . . .

PAUL: We *are* drugs.

JOE: And that's where the title of that song you and I wrote came from.

PAUL: Right, right. You know, I suppose I meant "our bodies are made up of chemicals . . ."

After the interview, the newly reconstituted Joe Hall and the Continental Drift played "Nos Hablos Telefonos," one of the band's most famous tunes. It was just like old times, except that George played the guitar, as he has for some reason abandoned the keyboards. The song was still programmed into my bass-playing fingers, since the group played it at every show we ever gave. Then I cleared off the stage, making room for J.P. Hovercraft, my bass-playing successor, and Jill said, "Come on, I'll take you back to Toronto, and we can go to the hospital."

Now, I don't mean to be giving such a matter-of-fact account, but it was this little setback that put me on the real journey. At the hospital, a doctor poked a long needle into my back and drew off another three litres of fluid. I wasn't even admitted on that occasion. I spent most of the night in emergency, then managed to convince the doctor in charge to let me loose. Not that I was developing an intense hatred of hospitals or anything. Quite to the contrary, I was reforming my opinion of them, which had previously been quite low. When Richard was in hospital, for example, I only visited on a couple of occasions (one of which he slept through), and I found the experience depressing. I even announced to some friends that, when my time came, I was going to eschew the institution, because I didn't want to be in a hospital, and I didn't want people to come visit me in a hospital. I think now what I was really reacting to was the fact that Richard was dying, cancer slowly draining his life force. Hospitals are pretty amazing, and the people employed there, everyone from the surgeons to the guys who pushed me down the hallways to radiology, are overworked and caring. But I managed to get sprung on that occasion, sometime around dawn, and I went back to the house on First Avenue.

Dr. Li was concerned that I'd had to have more fluid removed. The chemotherapy, she said, might well compromise my immune system, and if I had to get tapped again during the process, I was in danger of infection. Maybe, she suggested, we should deal with the fluid before starting the chemo. Dr. Li thought I should talk to Dr. Simone, the thoracic surgeon. "You could see if he's in," she said. "His office is just upstairs." We—my health crew, Dorothy, Jill, and Marty, were there with me—went to the third floor, and, remarkably, Dr. Simone told us to come on in. He listened to what we had to tell him and scheduled me for a pleurodesis.

Listen, if I'm being dreadfully boring about all this, please just toss the book in a corner. I hate it when people go into detail about their surgical procedures, but I do think this one is reasonably interesting, and it's not one I knew anything about. Indeed, I still knew very little about it long after it was done to me. But basically, after I was put under, Dr. Simone punched a hole through my side and stuck in a tube that would drain off the fluid. See, fluid collecting in the pleural cavity was my big problem, essentially crushing my left lung. That was the havoc my tumour was wreaking. The issue was not the fluid, because we all produce it, but the tumour not allowing me to reabsorb it. So, having drilled a hole in my side and stuck in a tube, Dr. Simone then blasted in talcum powder.

That's my understanding of things, anyway. I have learned that doctors like to speak by analogy, and they especially like visual aids. For example, we had asked Dr. Simone why he couldn't simply remove the tumour. He was sitting behind the desk in his office as he answered this, and he immediately scanned his desk top, seeking the means of illustration. He picked up the mouse for his computer. "Paul's tumour isn't like this, you know, where it can just be removed." He then picked up the blotter pad. "It's like this, you see. It's thin, but spread out." (I believe the technical term, which I first heard from Dr. Frazier, but didn't inquire about, having had my concentration scuppered sometime around, "It's cancer, lung cancer...," is "sessile." Mosslike.) When explaining the pleurodesis, Dr. Frazier found nothing suitable on his desk top, so instead he rubbed the palms of his hands together. "Imagine that you have two plates of glass, and you put sand in between them. At a certain point, friction would cause them to"—Dr. Simone stopped his rubbing abruptly.—"stick together."

This is what was done to me. The procedure was successful. I knew, we all knew, that it would not hold indefinitely. But it did give me a little time to consider how best to proceed. Margit Asselstine, a woman I've known for a very long time, did some work on me. I'm not sure exactly what sort of work; she used her hands a great deal but tended not to touch me. Anyway, I felt much better after seeing her. And one thing she told me was, "Paul, you have a lot of health still in your body. And there's a lot of health in the world that you can draw on."

Yeah, I thought. I *am* healthy. As funny as it might sound, it occurred to me the one thing I had going for me was that I was healthy. Big and burly. I began to wonder why, exactly, I was so eager to make myself sick. Especially since the chemo was palliative. Especially if it might only buy me a couple of months. Suppose those months were February and March. Here in Ontario, that might not seem such a great gift.

46

Okay, thought I, let's have a re-think. I assembled the health team. We conferred. The decision was to forgo chemotherapy, at least until I found myself in trouble. In the meantime, there were shows to play, songs to write, people to see, and places to visit. I may only have a year, I thought, but it's going to be one hell of a year.

And it revolved around music.

CHAPTER

[**3**]

I'M GOING to continue detailing my musical education. Condensing it to a few pages, however, whilst useful in terms of pacing, fails to adequately convey the time given over to the process. I spent months, maybe even years, sitting in the basement. It might take, say, a week to learn a song, which involved much lifting and replacing of the phonograph needle on the platter. Even though I tried to do this gingerly, I purchased a new needle practically every other day. After the week spent learning a song, another week would be devoted to playing that song, executing it with pride and exultation.

It is during this early period in a musician's life, I believe, that he or she acquires a unique cluster of predilections. Some tricky little licks, through a quirk of anatomy or some other manifestation of blind luck, come more easily to the fingers. A chord change affects some dim recess of the soul. Why? Who knows? Some combination of personal memory and cultural resonance, probably. And these become a songwriter's personal memes, the basis upon which the compositions that lie far ahead in the future are built.

Are you familiar with memetics? I hope you are. Otherwise, what I'm about to say may confuse you. The "meme," according to Richard Brodie, author of the book *Virus of the Mind*, is "the basic building block of culture in the same way the gene is the basic building block of life." "Memes," Brodie states, "are the building blocks of your mind, the programming of your mental 'computer.'" The concept of the meme was invented by Richard Dawkins, so there is an easily discernible neo-Darwinian context. Let us say that caveman Og, beating a hollow log with a bone, hits upon a rhythm that has a curious appeal, not only to himself but to the others gathered nearby. This makes Og more sexually desirable than Nood, who insists on emphasizing the first and third beat and never approaches what we might call ur-funk. In these terms, rock stars are the epitome, using music to make themselves sexually attractive and then disseminating their genes far and wide. Indeed, this is how Charles Darwin accounted for the existence of music in the first place, likening it to the peacock's lurid herl. I also like to imagine that musical memes contribute to the evolution of music itself, that they shape it to become increasingly beautiful and stirring. My thinking here has very little scientific credibility, so take it with a grain of salt. But, for example, I believe I have identified one such "meme," a small musical idea: five-one-two, so-do-re (in solfège). To me, that little phrase has deep resonance; it states the interval of the fifth, the note that splits the octave in half, and then it launches into the unknown, leaving us without solid musical footing. That meme serves as the beginning of Handel's "For Unto Us a Child Is Born." It turns up several times in Brahms's work; think of the lonely oboe that announces the arrival of the lovesick piano in the First Concerto. I myself use it all the time.

So, as I've said, every songwriter has his or her memes. A Randy Newman song has a distinctive quality. Newman is from a musical family—his uncles Lionel, Alfred, and Emil all wrote music for the motion pictures—and Newman's memes (the intervals and inversions he chooses, his chord structure, the melodic intervals) come from a very particular place. To my way of thinking, they have the same poignancy as, say, the musical memes of Charles Ives or Aaron Copland. Newman's success has as much to do with the genius of his lyrics as anything else, I should add, but we're not discussing lyrics, we're discussing memes.

Memetics were at play during my own formative years, then, but any kind of payoff was still years in the distance. PQ's People failed in our quest for global domination. Joel became distracted by the double bass, anyway. He'd been allowed into the music program at our junior high school, shunted into the string section. When asked by the teacher which instrument he'd prefer, Joel pointed at the hulking, oversized viol standing in the corner. It is my opinion that his reasoning proceeded thus: that thing over there is big; if I were a guy who played that thing, I would therefore myself be big, despite all the physical evidence, which would indicate that I am kind of a shrimpy little fella. So he began to play the double bass right then, and indeed, he has not played anything else since.[1]

As much as I came to love the Beatles—hold on, I should admit something. In 1964, at the height of Beatlemania, I was in Grade 6, and there were two distinct factions. There were those kids who felt that the Beatles were the greatest thing ever. And there were those kids, of which I was one, who felt that the Dave Clark Five were every bit as good, if not a little bit better. Yeah, I know. I have a history of such decisions. For a while, I preferred Donovan to Bob Dylan. Let me explain that I've always admired tuneful singing over idiosyncratic intoning or stylization. I can't really defend this stance, as it has caused me to dismiss many artists that I should have paid attention to. I have made a handful of good choices over the years, too, however. My favourite of all the British groups were (was?) the Animals. True, Eric Burdon bombilated more than he sang, but even then I could recognize the magnificence of his pipes.

But though the Beatles set the tone in the sixties, I soon came to realize I had trouble harmonizing. I was pudgy, saddled with spectacles, and long hair exacerbated my acne. They didn't seem to have any groovy clothes in the Husky section of the children's clothing department at Eaton's. To top it all off, when I was fifteen my mother died, which made me surly and silent.

---

1 My brother has never, in his life, had a job other than playing the bass as a soloist or in various orchestras and chamber groups. I myself have had several jobs. For example, for a while in my early twenties I was a tire-stacker. There were these tractor tires, and they needed to be shipped to various parts of Canada, so it was necessary that they be stacked in freight cars. My partner and I stacked 'em right to the top of the car, which I think made for a fourteen-tractor-tire-deep stack.

DOROTHY MADE an appointment for me to see Xiaolan. Actually, several people had suggested that I see Xiaolan, as she has a reputation for healing that is formidable. Moreover, Xiaolan is attached to the literary world, because she has written books (one was co-authored by my friend Marni Jackson) that were published by Anne Collins at Random House (my fiction editor). The short story on Xiaolan Zhao is that, although she trained in and first practised Western medicine, she decided that it was wrong to turn her back on more ancient practices. Acupuncture, massage, herbs, and unguents: that's the kind of medicine she advocates. So off Dorothy and I went to the clinic, a squat brownstone on Prince Arthur Avenue staffed by many women wearing starched white lab coats. On my first visit, I was examined by Xiaolan, who declared that she could help, but that my health ultimately depended on myself. Then she proceeded to work on me, a process that involved things like sticking her fingers up my nose and in my ears and placing pins in various parts of my body, including the top of my head. Xiaolan never announced her intention of doing any specific thing, so for that hour I was in a state of constant surprise, even shock. I've been back a number of times since, and this is a trait shared by the doctors there. They simply do things to you, things like laying a forearm to the small of your back with the sudden intensity of Sweet Daddy Siki or the Sheik. One practitioner, Mariko, did mutter something one time, apparently asking permission. I didn't quite catch what she said, but it was something about "cups."

"Good for drawing out toxins," she said. "Is that all right?"

"Sure," I shrugged. Or made a gesture as close to a shrug as I could, given that I was lying face down on a massage table, my face pushed through the hole, and had needles sticking out of my arms, my ears, and the back of my neck. Mariko busied herself. I could hear the tinkling of glass, I could hear her arranging things on a trolley, I could hear the trolley approach. There was the sound of flame, as though Mariko were lighting up a smoke (which I thought unlikely), and then suddenly a perfect circle of my back fat was sucked up by some concentration of Hell. I barely had time to scream before it happened again, and again. It happened approximately thirty times; that's how many little glass bowls Mariko drew the air out of (that was what the flame was all about) and then adhered to my flesh.

It was one of the most intense things I've ever experienced. As far as my back is concerned, it's number one on the list. The next day my back was vividly patterned with circles in a range of purples from light to royal. I felt not so well the next day, and then better, and then pretty well indeed. So perhaps the cupping did achieve the aim of drawing out toxins, and perhaps the many pills Xiaolan gives me (the dosages are along the lines of "eight pills, three times a day") effectively battle the tumour. To be honest, I really don't know. But I do know this: I like the attitude Chinese medicine has about cancer. They don't treat it, as Westerners do, as though it were the boogeyman hiding under the cellar stairs. They don't panic when the word is mentioned and start looking for the rat poison. As Xiaolan explained it, cancer represents an imbalance, and imbalances can be addressed. Except, you know, I have a bit of a hard time finding balance. Take my diet, for example.

Xiaolan wanted me to see her nutritionist, Christina Gordon, so I went along again to the clinic on Prince Arthur. This time, I brought Rebecca Campbell with me. Rebecca has gathered great critical acclaim as a solo artist and songwriter, and she also sings and plays percussion for Porkbelly Futures. It was early July by now, and the band was scheduled to begin a two-week, ten-date tour of the Maritimes in less than a week. I knew that I was going to need a great deal of help on the nutrition front. Rebecca is pretty health-conscious, and she is receptive to non-traditional ideas. Which is to say, she's not going to turn and hightail it just because something is a little wacky. And Christina was a little wacky. She was vivacious and very pregnant, and I liked her instantly, but she was flitting around some pretty distant lightbulbs. For example, she practised "oracular" medicine (I think that's what I heard), which involved me lying on a table and her waving some object toward my head. She placed and replaced small vials between my fingers, apparently trying to determine which particular holistic medicine my body was receptive to.[2] She also told me what I should and shouldn't be eating.

Kale came up. Kale comes up a lot in the context of what people with cancer should be eating. Just for the record, I'm not convinced kale is even edible, but it was duly listed (Rebecca was inscribing madly in her notebook) along with other leafy greens. Beef was out, but somehow lamb survived the cut. No dairy, although I could eat goat cheese. I asked about spicy food, and Christina shook her head, but I thought that was a little arbitrary, or perhaps she hadn't really understood the question. Rebecca inquired about various concoctions that she might render with her juicer, and Christina told her what vitaminic additives would make the stuff sparkle. "I know there's a big difference between what I want you to do

---

2 As things turned out, it was the rather archaic-sounding "aurum metallicum."

and compliance," said Christina. "Sometimes the joy factor outweighs the health factor."[3] I thought that statement evidenced much wisdom.

"And when you're on tour," said Christina, "try to have some fun."

"Oh," Rebecca assured her, "we have fun, all right."

"You've got to have more fun than you've ever had. Remember, the tumour hates laughter. It hates laughter, and it loves fear."

That's something I still say to myself, even as I realize that I'm out too late and have had too many drinks and really should be home in bed.

The tumour hates laughter.

Christina had, prior to her somewhat draconian pronouncements on diet, asked me a lot of questions about my family life. She wanted to know if my parents were alive, and I reported no. My father died suddenly, of a heart attack, at age seventy-six. My mother died of a cerebral hemorrhage when both she and I were very young. "It sucks that you don't have parents," Christina said. "And it especially sucks that your mother died when you were so young. You know, in Chinese medicine, the emotion associated with the lungs is sadness. I'm not saying that you have lung cancer because your mother died, but I am saying the two things may be connected."

Hmm. Well, it certainly was when I began smoking in earnest. I'd smoked prior to that—we all smoked—but after my mother died I declared my affection for Player's Plain (non-filtered cigarettes—"dead-ends," as we put it) and puffed away with vigour and enthusiasm. Or maybe anger is the right

---

3 Which, to me, meant only one thing: suicide chicken wings were back on the list!

word. And maybe I was doing it because the inhalation, sharp and painful, hit the sadness bulls-eye that was my lungs.

ONE DAY at school, soon after my mother's funeral, I was approached in the hallway by Paul D. I knew Paul from my childhood, since he and his brother were the most notorious ne'er-do-wells in the area. His brother was worse. At least, his brother got into more trouble—perhaps he simply got caught more, Paul having a half-step on him in a foot race—and spent a lot of time in reform school. (They don't seem to have reform schools anymore. What happened to them? I imagine derelict buildings perched high upon barren hills, the sounds of lashes still echoing.) Yes, Paul was a hood, although with the British Invasion he had let his hair grow long and started doing huge quantities of drugs. Paul D. had always liked me, which I reciprocated, because he had a sunny disposition and a great sense of humour, and if I were friends with Paul D. it meant I couldn't actually be the lard-assed wimp that I appeared to be. So, as I say, this boy, unshaven and whorly-eyed, came up to me in the hallway and said, "Hi, Paul. What's new?"

"My mother died," I informed him.

"Oh." Paul nodded, momentarily sombre. Then he asked, "What on the bright side?"

Paul invited me over to his place. For reasons that I can't explain—I mean, I don't know the explanation myself—he and his brother, John, had their own apartment. I don't know where the parents were. It's possible that Paul and John were remittance men, the black sheep of some blue-blooded family, sent to live in the wilds of Scarborough and provided with a stipend every month. All I know is, the brothers shared an apartment in a high-rise at the corner of Victoria Park and Lawrence. It is there we repaired to after school, or, actually, a couple of hours before "after school" officially began.

I remember that the place wasn't a pigsty, which was impressive. Mind you, there wasn't a lot there, a dining room table and some chairs. I sat down while Paul fetched refreshment.

"Where's John?"

"Oh, well, you know," answered Paul from the small kitchen area. I heard a small "pop." "He's gone away for a little while."

Paul D. returned with a bottle of wine, two greasy articles of stemware threaded through his fingers. "A fine Beaujolais," he announced, pouring me a glass. "Cheers. Sorry about your mom."

They say an experience shared by alcoholics is that with the first taste of hooch, a tremendous sense of wellbeing descends. I did not have that experience, not at all. The first two sips were bitter, and I barely managed to swallow them back. With that third sip, though, I was enveloped by a cloud of fluffy, muzzy contentment.

I'd found a new hobby.

The other thing that happened around that time was that my brother Tony fetched home a record album, a sampler from a company called Elektra. The label was largely dedicated to folk artists, and very good ones, too, people like Tom Rush and Tim Buckley. The record company was also making a stab at the new young audience of hippies with the Doors and the Lovin' Spoonful (a group I thought the world of), but what really intrigued me on that Elektra sampler was the Paul Butterfield Blues Band. They played music unlike much else

I'd heard. For one thing, that bullying rhythm was back, the same beast I'd encountered in Conrad's basement. It grabbed me by the collar and shook me back and forth. And over-top of that rhythm there was this electrified keening, young Mike Bloomfield pulling teeth out of a beat-up old Telecaster. The harmonica, as played by Butterfield, didn't sound like a human voice; it sounded way more human than that, the howl of a beggar outside the Pearly Gates. Not only that, but photographs of the band showed them to be pot-bellied louts, with greasy hair and nicotine-stained fingers. Some still retained their Brylcreem-sculpted greaser 'dos. A couple were even black. Musically, fashion-wise, even as a lifestyle, this seemed a reasonable alternative to a pudgy young anti-social fellow like me. I became a fifteen-year-old hard-drinking, hard-smoking bluesman from Don Mills, Ontario.

There is a great deal of musicological research focussed on the origins of the blues, how it all has to do with field hands exchanging calls and responses as they went about their back-breaking labour.

"It fucking hurts—"

"Really, really fucking hurts—"

"When we bend down!"

"It fucking hurts when we bend down."

I suppose that's glib, and I don't mean to be, but I think I'm pointing, if vaguely, at something of a truth, that the blues tend to be songs of complaint. (The other side of that, the hope for a better life, is reflected by the blues' slightly more elegant and refined sister, gospel. The two were reunited in the fifties by people like Ray Charles and Sam Cooke, who sang gospel music with lyrics that reflected more secular concerns.) Musicologists assert that the call-and-response tradition was prevalent in many areas of Africa, where the slaves brought to the U.S. originated. They likewise point out that an essential influence on the blues was the European music of the slave owners. James Campbell notes in *The Picador Book of Blues and Jazz* that the *aab* rhyming scheme found in most blues, Nick Gravenites's "Born in Chicago," for instance,

> I was born in Chicago, nineteen-forty-one.
> Born in Chicago, nineteen-forty-one.
> My father told me, "Son, get yourself a gun."

is also present in many old ballads that predate the arrival of the first slave in the New World:

> Polly, pretty Polly, won't you come along with me?
> Polly, pretty Polly, won't you come along with me?
> Before we get married, some new love to see.

There's also a commonality between the two kinds of music in their physical urgency. The ancient balladeer seemed every bit as anxious to get his rocks off as the most hormone-addled bluesman.

A songster was, originally, a little book that contained songs—ballads, "coon" songs (sorry, but that's what the musicians themselves called them), ditties popular with the hoi polloi. The booklets had titles like *The Forget Me Not Songster* and *The Arkansas Traveller Songster*. Sometime during the nineteenth century, the term "songster" was gradually applied to the itinerant black musician (actually, the parlance of the time was "musicianer") who went from place to place clutching a songster in his hand. A songster would have in his repertoire a few blues songs—the twelve-bar variety, with the inviolate *aab* rhyming scheme—but he was by no means limited to the blues, nor would he typically care to be. The esteemed critic Robert Palmer noted in his book *Deep Blues* that Charley Patton, later known as the father of Delta blues, was a songster of catholic propensities, singing "blues, white hillbilly songs, nineteenth century ballads, and other varieties of black and white country dance music with equal facility." The focus on twelve-bar blues, and its association with black artists in the first half of the twentieth century, is in many ways the result of rampant commercialism. To be blunt, the owners of the "race record" companies, who were white, believed that the blues would sell better than that other stuff.

To be fair, the "race record" concept is not quite as reprehensible as it might seem. Race records did allow for the preservation and dissemination of a vital part of African-American culture. Black artists were among the first people to be recorded on the newfangled talking machines. Sometime in the late 1880s, George Washington Johnson recorded his trademark tunes, "The Whistling Coon" and "The Laughing Song." The reason I'm a little vague on the dates is that in those early days, each performance was captured on its own cylinder. So Johnson recorded those songs as many as fifty times a day. He was sufficiently big-lunged that he could whistle and laugh into five recording horns at once. The legend of how his recording career began is telling. Johnson was on the Staten Island Ferry, whistling, and Thomas Edison happened to hear him.[4] Edison invited Johnson to come to his laboratory

---

4 It likely wasn't Edison, rather a representative of the Metropolitan Phonograph Company, which is why I referred to it as a "legend." Legends are, of course, always better than the truth.

to make some recordings, and he offered to pay him twenty cents per two-minute song. Over time, those fees constituted a healthy income for Johnson, a man born into slavery. For Edison, and men like him, it was chump change. There was much more money to be made by selling the cylinders.[5]

Nick "the Greek" Gravenites was not born in 1941, despite the assertion in the song lyrics quoted above, although he *was* born in Chicago. Gravenites was born three years before that, in the Brighton Park section of the city. His father died when he was eleven, and his mother mourned for the next ten years, black-clad and intoning her sorrow in the traditional, melismatic manner (changing the pitch of a single syllable; an example would be the bellowing we do at Christmas when we sing the "Gloria" of "Angels We Have Heard On High"). Mrs. Gravenites was not able to manage her boy as Nick entered his teens, and he spent the next few years scuffling with the law. He was sent to a military academy—which seems to be the American equivalent of reform school, as far as I can tell—and finally, through the good graces of an English teacher, entered the University of Chicago. There he soon was involved with the U of C Folklore Society, and he became acquainted with some other misfit white kids eager to play music. There was one lad named Mike Bloomfield who was a whiz on the guitar, seemingly at home with every style, but obsessed with the blues. At the age of nineteen, Bloomfield became the manager of a club called the Fickle Pickle, and he would book all these old blues guys that no one except him had ever heard of.

5 Edison (if not Edison, then the well-fed white man in charge of things) didn't sell cylinders to the general public, of course, but rather to exhibitors, who would then go across the land setting up "phonograph parlors." People would listen through acoustical ear tubes and pay a fee for the privilege.

He would spend all night sitting right in front of them, listening and watching intently. And there was this other kid, nicknamed Bunky, who was not actually attending the university, because he was too young to do so. Bunky Butterfield was raised in an interracial section of Chicago. He was very popular with both his white and his black neighbours, because he was a likeable kid and he could play the hell out of a harmonica. It was these kids, along with a couple of other friends, Elvin Bishop and Charlie Musselwhite, who spearheaded the blues movement of the early sixties.

Oh, I know, I know, Keith Richards, Mick Jagger, and Brian Jones were similarly blues-obsessed, but they only had access to the records. The Chicago contingent had access to the old blues guys. They could see and sit in with musicians like Muddy Waters, Howlin' Wolf, Junior Wells, and Otis Rush. I think I could argue convincingly that this made them more authentic. At any rate, the Chicago guys, unlike their British counterparts, didn't achieve insane wealth or fame, both of which are challenges to a religious dedication to the blues. From 1963 to 1965, while the British Invasion was in full swing, the Butterfield band was labouring away at Big John's, a club on Chicago's North Side.

I will say this on behalf of those Britishers, they did acknowledge their debt to those old fellows. They made sure that royalties were directed toward their influences. But well they might. "(I Can't Get No) Satisfaction" is based on Muddy Waters's "I Can't Be Satisfied." Allan Moore, in his book *The Cambridge Companion to Blues and Gospel Music*, says the following: "[The Stones] substituted the banalities of American advertising for the blues male macho of the original. This loss of meaning in the British re-workings of American blues was a necessary part of the reason for its success with white audiences in the U.S."

BACK IN Canada, I was able to find myself some like-minded blues-obsessed friends.

In my first year of high school I met Patrick Murphy, who was (you'd never have guessed) of Irish heritage and bore the nickname "Murph." He was red-haired and bespectacled, and his nose bled all the time. Murph owned (and could play) an old Fender Precision Bass that had a bullet hole in it. There was a scrawny little kid named Gordie Paton who was apprenticing to become two things, an electrician and a chain-smoker. Gordie played the drums, adopting an odd and individual regimen that saw him practise at incredible velocity and volume. His attitude was, he could always slow and quiet down if he needed to.

And squalling away on the harp[6] was Kim Kotzma.

I was twelve and Kim was thirteen when we met. A group of young fellows had assembled to do something stupid—I believe the idea was to bust street lights with thrown rocks— and I backed away from the horde, *tsk*ing at the inanity of it all while inwardly bemoaning the fact that I had a weak arm.

---

6 The harmonica, I mean. Let me get a little technical. Pedantry is, after all, the function of footnotes, and it's not like you're reading them anyway. There are various types of harmonicas. There are the great big contraptions called "chromatic," because a little button on the side allows you to play half-tones. The kind popularized by Paul Butterfield et al. are smaller instruments designed to play in a specific key. There is a letter imprinted on the metal, let's say, G, which means that if you simply stick the thing in your mouth and blow, you will sound a melodious G chord. However, blues guys play "cross harp," that is, they sound the tonic by breathing in. That way they can perform all sorts of mouth and throat manoeuvres that would be unseemly in many other situations but allow the notes to be twisted and flattened in a soulful manner. So a G harmonica is actually a D blues harp. Get it?

At the same time, a much larger fellow, wearing skin-tight, bright red pants, pulled away as well. "What a bunch of tweezoks," he said. I wasn't certain that this guy was talking to me. For one thing, he was very, um, mature. Which is to say, he'd already been through puberty.[7] To me, puberty was still as distant as China. This guy, who was obviously allowed to dress himself however he wanted, seemed way too cool to be addressing me, but as he commenced walking I got caught up in his wake, and he didn't seem to mind. "Are they ever numb-nuts," he went on. "Don't they have anything better to do?"

The tweezoks and numbnuts really didn't have anything better to do. Then again, neither did we. We began to wander around the neighbourhood, and for the next few years we often did that in the middle of the night. Kim and I and Joel liked to "sneak out," which meant waiting until the household was fast asleep and then climbing out through the basement window. We could have gone out the back door, but that would have been no fun. And if there was nothing to do during the day, sample our suburban world at three o'clock in the morning.

It was my brother Tony who stuck an album in Kim's hand and said, "Listen to this guy named Paul Butterfield play the harmonica. You could do that." So Kim listened to the record, bought a Marine Band in the key of C, and discovered that he could, indeed, do that.

The group we eventually formed had a great name: Man-ure. I seem to remember we were originally called Mister

---

7   Indeed, he had the beginnings of a moustache, twenty-odd whiskers acting in valiant concord. As Kim matured further, his moustache essentially became a homuncu-lus, a creature that had grown happy and plump in the warm air wafting down from Kotzma's nostrils.

Manure and the Flounder Box Four, but that makes for a grand total of five, and whoever that mystery guy was, he either left the group or never existed. Manure did pretty well for a high school band. We played the blues—"I was born in Chicago, nineteen forty-one..."—and we were not without musical talent. Also, fuelled by precocious amounts of alcohol and drugs, we could behave rather outrageously, especially Kotzma, who, shirtless and bathed in sweat, was often inspired to leap from the little stages and either grab the rafters or belly-flop into the crowd. (And in those days, crowds tended not to catch stage-leapers.)

It was with Manure that I wrote my first song. It is possible that I invented a ditty prior to this, a little tune that I would whistle/hum, plunking out the accompaniment on a stringed instrument or the old, groaning piano in the basement. But it was with Manure that I first set out to write a song, or more specifically to co-write one. Murphy and I sat in his basement and collaborated. We also drank Old Man Murph's beer with insouciance. Murph claimed that he was allowed to do so, since his father's attitude was that allowing open alcohol consumption lessened the likelihood of more extreme clandestine imbibing. If so, Old Man Murph (that's what Patrick called him) was woefully mistaken.

I was fifteen or sixteen years old. I know that because the year was 1969, and I know it because the inspiration for our collaboration was the Who's *Tommy*, released that year. Tommy, of course, is a deaf, dumb, and blind boy. Our thought was to write a song about a boy hobbled by a condition that put him at odds with society, made of him an outcast and a pariah. Don't forget, Murph and I were boys born in the fifties, a time when medical authorities urged circumcision for reasons of cleanliness. To not be circumcised was therefore something of a rarity. Well, enough of trying to whitewash our manifest insensitivity. The song Murphy and I wrote had the title "Johnny No-Knob."

It was, believe it or not, quite a good song. It was not, as I remember it, formally a blues song, but it was certainly bluesy, and the inspiration we drew from the Who included a refrain complete with chiming power chords. When Manure played the song, the crowd would react with giddy, pumping enthu- siasm. Gordie Paton would pound the drums with unbridled energy, a cigarette clamped between pale lips. Murphy would grin and scan the crowd carefully, separating drug-addled cretins from mere morons. Kotzma would hurl himself into the crowd. And I would concentrate on my hands, because I have ever been withdrawn and inward-looking. Perhaps if I'd hurled myself with my buddy Kotzma, my life would have been completely different.

I saw the Butterfield Band—which was an amorphous creature, the personnel changing constantly to feature increasingly virtuosic guitarists—many times as a teenager, whenever they played Toronto. At least, whenever they played a concert or a festival. If they played a venue that was licensed to sell liquor, I was unable to attend, not yet having attained the age of majority. I consciously avoid the phrase "too young to drink," because I was, naturally, drinking all the time. Murph and I were devoted neobibes. We would hang around the parking lot at the local LCBO store, and when we spied a likely candidate—a fellow of say, twenty-two years of age, recently paroled from a penal institution—we would approach with the following proposition: We'll give you some money, you buy us some booze, and in return... Oh, wait a sec, it wasn't really a proposition at all. The guy never got any-thing out of the deal, except for, perhaps, a faint nostalgia for his own ill-spent youth. He would exit the store and give us the provender which, if Murph and I had money, might be a case of beer, but was more often than not a bottle of Four Aces.

I suspect that the truth-in-advertising board would insist, nowadays, that Four Aces label itself as a "wine-like bever-age." Maybe even a "beverage-like substance." All we knew about it was, it contained alcohol and it was cheap, namely, a bottle cost one dollar and five cents. "Come alive for a dollar five" was the refrain chanted by the fifteen-year-old bluesmen from Don Mills, Ontario, although I will tell you that Murph actually lived in Scarborough, which is a slightly better place for a bluesman to be from.

Despite my behaviour—the imbibing of Four Aces, the smoking of Players dead-ends—I had failed to become a hard-ened and seedy-looking bluesman. I looked years younger than my age and possessed such chubbiness of cheek that my nickname was, throughout my adolescence, Cherub.

At any rate, I went to see the Butterfield Band at a place we used to have here in Toronto, the Rock Pile, and unbeknownst to me, there were three other boys there who will play impor-tant roles in this story. One was a guy called Marty Worthy, whom I sort of knew. He was a year ahead of me in school, but he was friends with my next-door neighbour, Isobel, so I saw him every now and again. I had even visited Marty once when he was in hospital. Marty was there for several months when he was fifteen, having steel rods implanted in his back to deal with his scoliosis. Marty could play drums and sing; I knew that because I'd seen two of his groups perform at local sock-hops. The first group was called Marty's Martians, and they were a lightweight, poppy ensemble. After that, Marty played in an R&B group called the System. So Marty was there at that Butterfield concert, but I guess I just didn't see him, because I would have said hello. Also at the concert was a fellow named Chas Elliott. Although I didn't know him yet, I'm willing to bet I saw him, because Chas was (and is) a tall man, and would have loomed above the crowd. Chas played the bass, the big bull fiddle, and was studying at the conservatory. And also at the Butterfield gig, a fellow named Stuart Laughton, whom I learned in later years was pressed up against the apron of the stage snapping photographs. Stuart came from a family of musicians, and he was applying himself to the trumpet. As we shall see, his skills and interests in fact covered vast tracts of instrumental and stylistic ground.

KIM KOTZMA disappeared from our lives as we neared the eighteen-year-old mark. Murph, Gord, and I soldiered on. Manure persisted as a trio, and occasionally we'd find a fourth, although never someone who was willing, let alone eager, to fling themselves into the rafters. Kim drifted around, did some jail time on a drug-related charge, ended up in Calgary, Alberta, where he became a landscaper. It was in Calgary that I reconnected with Kim, because during the year of 1987 I spent a great deal of time there, writing a book about the Canadian Olympic hockey team. (As you might recall, the 1988 Winter Games were held in Calgary.) I stayed with Kim and his then-girlfriend and any number of animals, many of which—but certainly not all—were Kotzma's own pets. He came to visit in Toronto when my first daughter was born, and I know that because I have photographic evidence: Kotzma holding Carson in the palms of his hands, hugging her to his face, Carson grimacing because she was thus brought into contact with the creature that was Kim's 'stache. But between those two events—sometime between those events—Kim called with the news that he'd been diagnosed with multiple sclerosis. He spent a long time explaining what MS was, which he did with a chatty matter-of-factness.

Whenever book tours took me to Calgary, I had visited Kim, who by then had hooked up with a woman named Deborah. We would laugh and drink and get into a little trouble here and there, and sometimes I'd notice that Kim was walking stiffly, but I didn't think anything of it. For one thing, Kim had always been ridiculously healthy, possessed of one of those muscular bodies with a negative fat percentage. When the crowds failed to catch him after a stage-leap, he would bounce back to his feet without missing a beat. Now, he told me, he and Deborah were moving to Arizona, where the climate would be kinder to his condition.

After that our contact was mostly telephonic. And I will admit, with a certain amount of shame, that our contact was largely one-sided, with Kim leaving messages on my machine. "Okay, brother," he'd say. "Just wanted you to know that I was thinking about you. I love you, and we'll go from there."

I did go to visit Kim in Arizona, in the fall of 2007. He and Deborah had a place high upon a mountain—or a mesa, or some massive swelling of the earth's crust—near a place called Rio Rico. Through my guest room window I could see, first, a charming little patio area, rustic and treed and filled with birds that were, to my Ontario eyes and ears, wonderfully exotic. After the garden the land fell away, and it moved in great waves, vast and green and darkened by clouds' shadows; *High Chaparral* country.

Kim had by this time lost the ability to walk, and he rode around the property on a bright red scooter. He was reluctant to use his wheelchair, feeling that would be somehow giving up on his legs, which he was not willing to do, even though they had clearly given up on him. Still, Kim remained pretty hale. As he put it when I first laid eyes on him, "What, were you expecting a worm with a head on it?"

On Canadian Thanksgiving, we deep-fried a turkey and watched an American football game. After that, we sat out on the patio and talked. Kim had a bottle of tequila in the basket of his ride, and every so often he would pull it out, uncap it, and take a long draw. Myself, I drank beer[8] and watched the night fall. I mentioned a fellow we'd known in high school whom I'd seen recently, a fellow who was rather bitter that his musical career hadn't panned out.

Kim tilted his head, bewildered. "He's bitter about that?"

I shrugged. "Sure."

"That's weird," Kim said, truly not able to comprehend this. "I just figure life moves along." He pulled on his tequila. "I played in some bands, you know, in other places, and sometimes we got it going pretty good, but if it didn't work out, that was okay by me. There was a time in my life when I was good at music. And I'll always be thankful to your family. You guys introduced me to a world that I would never have

---

8 Oh, I forgot to mention something during the nutrition section earlier: Christina outlawed beer. Good luck.

known anything about. But then that was over. And I became a landscaper, and I was good at that." Kim stared at the black shapes of the mountains. "Now I'm good at living in a desert."

I believe it was the American novelist, poet, outdoorsman, and gourmand Jim Harrison who called bitterness "the writer's black lung disease," but musicians are likewise susceptible. There are some ameliorating circumstances. There are more opportunities, to be blunt, for second-rateness as a musician. There are Holiday Inns across the continent, and each has a little lounge, and a rock'n'roll wannabe (even a former rock'n'roll star) can ride out years and years playing stale music and drinking cheap shots. I know that sounds like a recipe for bitterness (and I'm certain that in many cases it is) but the very act of playing music is—sometimes in defiance of all odds—uplifting.[9] At three o'clock in the morning, you might play a lick with such poise and rightness that the drunk at table fourteen lifts his soggy head from the Formica and grins crookedly. But in both professions, writing and music, a practitioner stands about as much chance of real success as does a sperm cell. And there are no pre-established hallmarks of success. You don't get a raise after two years of belonging to the Musicians' Union. Indeed, you usually get fined by the union for taking a non-union gig. The only thing to gauge yourself by is how well other people are doing. The most visible people are doing way, way better than you, and the result is bitterness.

It did my heart good to hear my old buddy Kim talk the

9 In fact, this is the first plank in the platform of my somewhat idiosyncratic musical-healing therapy.

way he did. Multiple sclerosis is a horrible, horrible disease. But in many ways, bitterness is worse. Bitterness, say the wise men, is like drinking poison and expecting someone else to die.

ONE THING that has to be done after a diagnosis like mine is the calling of people.[10] People have to be called, and one has to say, "How's it going? Good. How's the wife? Good. Okay, listen, I've got cancer..."

You know what? People are *great*. I don't mean they're understanding or empathetic or anything like that. I mean they're great, they're fucking wonderful. Tell them you're sick, and you will receive such a warm, heartfelt response that you will be, like me, stupefied and stymied. It seems to me now that all most human beings are doing is waiting for someone to tell them they are in need of care and kindness, because those things are certainly forthcoming.

But there was one call I didn't want to make, and that was to my friend Kotzma. I knew Kim was—as I suddenly was—dealing with eternity sitting on his doorstep like a rolled-up newspaper. I postponed the call for far too long, three weeks or more. But that was a mistake, and I knew it seconds after Kotzma answered the phone. He was, as always, full of good advice. "Tell the people you love that you love them," Kim said. "Every chance you get. End every conversation with 'I love you.' Except, you know, when you're talking to someone you don't love."

Even so, after that I missed many of his phone calls, and I

---

10 It would be unfair of me not to mention that Marty, Jill, and Dorothy made a great many, maybe even most, of these phone calls.

was not good at returning them. It's a lame excuse, but my life got rather out of hand. Undaunted, Kim would leave his regular message: "I was thinking about you, hope you're doing well. I love you, and we'll go from there."

One night my phone rang at two o'clock in the morning. I was in bed, on the houseboat, and I noted the number. I thought, "Well, Kim's had a tug or two too many on his tequila bottle. I'll call him back in the morning." But I didn't. Instead, I went out to a recording studio with Porkbelly Futures to start work on our third album. So it was not until dinnertime that I listened to the message. It was Kim's wife, Deborah, and she was informing me that Kim had passed away that day.

CHAPTER

[4]

WOODY GUTHRIE died of Huntington's disease, a neurodegenerative disorder. The disease is progressive and fatal, and Guthrie was hospitalized for the last decade of his life. One of his regular visitors at the Brooklyn State Hospital was a young musician from Hibbing, Minnesota, who idolized Guthrie and the things he represented. As *Time* magazine reported in November 1963, "The tradition of Broonzy[1] and Guthrie is being carried on by a large number of disciples, most notably a promising young hobo named Bob Dylan... He dresses in sheepskin and a black corduroy Huck Finn cap, which covers only a small part of his long, tumbling hair... He delivers his songs in a studied nasal that has just the right clothespin-on-the-nose honesty to appeal to those who most deeply care." Bob Dylan is going to turn up at key points in this narrative, as you will see, and

---

1 The reference is to Big Bill Broonzy, a bluesman from Bolivar County, Mississippi, who was popular with white audiences and helped spearhead the folk revival.

this is an appropriate moment in my own musical history to bring him in.[2]

My friend Bobby G. and I entered into a brief business partnership when we were approximately twelve years old. I was twelve years old, anyway. Throughout my life, it's usually been the case that my friends are a little older than I, and I suspect this was the case with Bob. He was much taller, for one thing. He was much taller than most people, and there seemed to be no end in sight. Bobby's body quivered and sprouted upwards, as in those time-lapse photography segments depicting a tendril struggling toward the sun. He was curly haired and perpetually wore a loopy grin, as if he knew where something kind of disgusting was buried. But he was a nice guy, one of the nicest guys I've known in this lifetime, and the business partnership we formed was never fraught with any kind of suspicion or tension. Mind you, it was short-lived, and there was very little money involved. Sixty-nine cents, if I remember correctly, which is what a forty-five cost in those days.

Some of you may recall forty-fives, which were delightful in every way—discs of music seven inches in diameter, slipped into a plain paper envelope, with a circle cut out of the envelope so that the pertinent information on the label could be read. Except for that damn centre. Remember? The little records had a hole in the middle an inch across. That had something to do with some fucking competition between Columbia and RCA. I don't even pretend to understand it. All

---

2 I was surprised at how often I ended up writing about Dylan, in fact. As big a fan as I am, I hadn't realized quite how profound his influence was on the popular song in the last half of the last century. I mentioned this in an e-mail to my friend Roddy Doyle, who responded, "Thanks for the heads up about Dylan. I'll Google him."

I know is that it meant you had to go out and buy a piece of plastic, a "centre," as we Canadians would have it, in order to make the thing fit onto the turntable's spindle. (You could try to place the single on the turntable freehand, with geometric exactitude—but that method ensured, almost without fail, that the chart-toppers you were listening to wowed and drawled most unmusically.) Come to think of it, this may have been the origin of the partnership I established with Bob G.: he owned one of those yellow plastic centres.

Assuming that to be the case, on the day in question, Bob ponied up thirty-four cents and I made up the difference, giving us the requisite sixty-nine cents. My other contribution was my enthusiasm, because the whole thing was my idea. We took our sixty-nine cents and purchased "Like a Rolling Stone."

Dylan had been a constant in our household for two or three years. Tony brought home his albums—I recollect *The Freewheelin' Bob Dylan* in particular, with its iconic cover, Dylan walking the streets of New York with a girl clinging to his arm—and my father judged them not to be too bad—at least, he allowed them to be spun often and loudly. Dylan played folk music, simple and unadorned. He spat out the lyrics with smirking insolence, but this never seemed to deprive the words of their importance. It was the sixties, and the times were a-changing; people believed that the course of events could be redirected by the common will, and that this will could be affected profoundly by the song. By the protest song, to give it a label that today possesses a heartbreaking quaintness. Protest songs were so prevalent back then that they blasted through the air during the barbeques hosted by my parents and their friends, adults and teenagers alike singing along with zeal and piety.

I'm hard-pressed now to tell you exactly why I campaigned for Bob and me to purchase "Like a Rolling Stone." The song was just beginning its ascent of the music charts. It would eventually reach number two in the U.S. of A., the first popular song to break the three-minute rule.[3] Indeed, it smashed that rule to smithereens, being six minutes in length. I hadn't heard "Like a Rolling Stone" on the radio. I didn't have a radio. (There was some sort of receiver integrated into the hi-fi system in the living room, but it's not like I could take that to bed with me and try to pull in "Abilene," and that's the purpose of a radio, isn't it?) I suppose I might have gathered from overheard snippets of conversation between Tony and his friends that Bob Dylan had done something inappropriate. That he'd gone too far, in many people's view. I've always been intrigued with people who go too far. At any rate, that Saturday afternoon Bob G. and I took the bus to Eglinton Station, and then a train south to the Dundas subway station, where we effected the purchase at Sam the Record Man. We got back on the subway, rattled north, and took the bus back to the suburbs.

Bob had a kind of a den set up in his family's two-car garage. He had a turntable on his father's bench-saw, a

3 In 1930, in what many people consider one of the most important country blues sessions ever, Charley Patton, Son House, Willie Brown, and singer and pianist Louise Johnson recorded together at the Paramount studios in Grafton, Wisconsin. A significant aspect to that session has to do with the technical limitations of the era. As each number was played and sung, the music was etched—right then and there—onto a wax disc called the "matrix"—what we might now call a master, as it was thence used to create the stamper and the commercial copies. The matrix spun at a speed of seventy-eight rpm, and a ten-inch disc (the most dependable size, less breakable than bigger versions, which did exist) could hold a little over three minutes of music. So the musicians were required to limit their performances to three minutes. That edict—this is my non-scholarly conjecture—affected the recording process long after the seventy-eight had gone the way of the dodo.

speaker wire leading to a couple of cabinets suspended in the corners. Many of my friends were good at making speaker cabinets. Of all the differences between my daughters' generation and my own, this often strikes me as the most dramatic. We wouldn't have wanted to put anything called "buds" into our ears, no matter what kind of fidelity they promised. Rather, we enjoyed pulling paper cones and dusty magnets out of derelict consoles, slapping together a housing out of plywood, and settling the surround into the baffle as best we could. Bob G. possessed some talent in woodworking, so his cabinets didn't rattle even when we cranked the volume really high.

And we cranked the volume *really* high. We listened to that song maybe seventy-eight times in a row. We took turns picking up the needle and placing it back on the spinning disc. We didn't say anything to each other, but occasionally we'd look into each other's eyes, checking to see if the other guy was going through the same thing.

To this day, I can't hear the opening strains of "Like a Rolling Stone" without experiencing a thrill, a realization that the world is suddenly about to become far more interesting than it was just moments before.[4]

I DON'T really have a clever segue into my new thematic material here, except that "Like a Rolling Stone" is, in my estimation, a great song, and it was on that day I decided one of the things I wanted to do with my life was write a great

4 Bruce Springsteen reported something similar. When he first heard the song, he recalled at Dylan's induction into the Rock and Roll Hall of Fame, "I was in the car with my mother listening to WMCA, and on came that snare shot that sounded like somebody had kicked open the door to your mind."

song. I can't say that I've done so, but I have taken a couple of good shots.

After the reception of the dread Dire Diagnosis, I began to think about the work I'd be leaving behind. I asked myself, "If I were to die tomorrow, would I be satisfied with my output?" Surprisingly, I thought my ten novels were fine. I felt no great urgency to start scribbling the masterwork that might ensure my immortality. None of my novels was particularly successful.[5] Still, I liked them well enough. I worked hard at them, and they are, for the most part, what I intended them to be. Likewise with my five books of what I sometimes refer to as "whimsical non-fiction." This memoir was uncompleted, and I was contractually obligated to submit a second draft, so that was on my to-do list, as I've said. There were also a couple of television projects I wanted to push as far as they could go, because I thought they were worthwhile and might provide some money for my family.

But my songwriting, that was a different story. I actually felt like I was maybe just getting good, that I was getting close to a place inside me where the words and the music could be easily accessed. I had become interested in combining musical forms with longer narrative, and without really being aware that I was doing so, had composed some *recitatifs* and *singspiels*. I was very proud of a couple of these, *Friendly!* and *Hey, Hollywood*. One of the things I liked best about these songs was that they were true, by which I mean factually precise and germane to my life. It comes back to what I was saying near the beginning of this little volume, that songs should be *about* something.

5   I'm speaking of commercial and critical success. On all other levels, they turned out okay.

One song running through my mind these days is "Tom Dooley." I suppose it's natural, under the circumstances, that I should be drawn to a refrain like "Poor boy, you're bound to die." I listened to that song a lot when I was a little boy, and it scared me shitless. Something truly wicked had happened up there on the mountain. "Tom Dooley" is based on the misadventures of a womanizing, banjo-picking Confederate soldier named Tom Dula, but the point here is not the song's historical accuracy. The point is that the balladeers used dark colours on a big canvas.

Here's another way of saying that. The musician Lou Reed, as a university student in Syracuse in the early 1960s, entered the sphere of influence of Delmore Schwartz, poet, alcoholic, and habitué of the White Horse Tavern.[6] Reed thereafter decided that the Song should have every bit as big a realm as the Novel, as great a scope. Lou Reed's songs are informed by a novelist's bravery and recklessness, and that's the spirit I determined I would emulate in what songwriting work of mine there was to come.[7]

I felt there was a song I needed to write, a song that would address, somehow, my bumping up against Death's Door. A phrase entered my mind. That's an accurate statement, since suddenly there were three words in my head that hadn't been there before. They weren't the culmination of any cud-chewing; those three simple words arrived all by themselves. We could debate whether they were shoved forward, like

6 Delmore Schwartz is also the model for Von Humboldt Fleisher in Saul Bellow's wonderful novel *Humboldt's Gift*.
7 One of the first manifestations of this was my inclusion of the phrase "twiddle with my dinky" in the song *Friendly!* Hardly a bold statement; still, many people are oddly irked and rankled by it.

small children, by the bureaucrats in some buried mental department. Or maybe inspiration is divine. I'm hedging my bets at this point. But those words—"all the stars"—came to me with unexpected clarity, and I believe I actually pulled on my chin as I wondered, "What's that supposed to mean?"

I allowed my novelistic sensibility free rein. I imagined a man—a quiet man, a nice man, a man who likely enjoys crossword puzzles and never did any real harm to anyone else— and I imagined him stepping outside, looking up, and seeing all the stars.

> But I walked outside, just after midnight...
> And I saw all the stars.

As I continued, it quickly became apparent that the man was missing someone, that his partner was no longer alive. In the final verse, he writes this person a letter, acknowledging the futility of the act. "Still," he intones with a shrug, "you do what you gotta do to survive." And then the man looks up at the sky again, seeing all those billions and billions of stars, essentially all of creation. It is a small miracle that such a tiny human act can reap such amazing benefit. It was a good song. I showed it to the rest of Porkbelly Futures. We added it to our repertoire just before we hit the road for the Maritimes.

OKAY—BACK TO Bob Dylan. When my brother's friends speculated about whether Dylan had "gone too far," they were, of course, referring to his appearance, on July 25, 1965, at the Newport Folk Festival.

It was Dylan's third consecutive appearance at the festival, and in the years previous, he had done exactly what was expected of him. He'd stood in front of a microphone—actually, two large radio-style microphones duct-taped together—and rendered his songs of protest. He'd invited Peter, Paul and Mary, Joan Baez, and the Freedom Singers to join him onstage as he sang "Blowin' in the Wind," accompanying himself and the others on his guitar, stiffly strummed and rudimentally fingered.

That summer, as in summers previous, Dylan spent a great deal of time in Woodstock, New York, staying at the home of his manager, Albert Grossman. I have no concrete evidence that he was indulging in pharmaceuticals—other than the fact that *everyone else in the world was*—but his writing was becoming increasingly, well, agitated. The husky-throated Baez, his girlfriend at the time, recalled, "Most of the month or so we were there, Bob stood at the typewriter in the corner of his room, drinking red wine and smoking and tapping away relentlessly for hours. And in the dead of night, he would wake up, grunt, grab a cigarette, and stumble over to the typewriter again."

One ignores at one's peril (isn't it hateful when one begins with "one," and one is therefore compelled to keep using "one"?) the former Robert Zimmerman's choice to rename himself "Dylan," after Dylan Thomas, the great and fabulously self-destructive Welsh poet. Zimmerman was inspired by the driven manner in which Thomas spun lyrical gold out of the dross of his day-to-day life. He was likewise inspired by French poets like Rimbaud and Baudelaire, and by the Surrealists, who allowed their thoughts to come forth freely and uncensored. I could say much about that school of thinking, but I believe the Surrealists' position is succinctly expressed by one of their visual arts counterparts, Salvador

Dali. "There is only one difference between a madman and me," he asserted. "I am not mad."

So it was in this frame of mind that Dylan had gone too far at the Newport Folk Festival in 1965. He was the Sunday night headliner; the act preceding him was Cousin Emmy, whose big tune was "Turkey in the Straw." After singing two songs acoustically, Dylan was joined onstage by Al Kooper and Barry Goldberg (on organ and piano), Sam Lay (drums), Jerome Arnold (bass), and the whiz kid from the Fickle Pickle, Mike Bloomfield.[8] And as he launched into "Maggie's Farm," there came—or so legend has it—a resounding chorus of catcalls and boos. "Sell out!" people shouted, and "Bring back Cousin Emmy!"

Dylan was startled, even shaken, by the response. After all, his most recent album, *Bringing It All Back Home*, had featured an acoustic side and an electric side. Some people claimed later that at least a few boos were directed at the very poor sound quality. Others said that the most vocal of the dissenters were backstage. Pete Seeger, who didn't like the music one little bit, reportedly announced, "If I had an axe, I'd cut the cable right now!" Festival board member Alan Lomax, likewise incensed, pleaded with the sound men to turn the volume down. Dylan and his band rushed through "Like a Rolling Stone" and "Phantom Engineer," a song that eventually became "It Takes a Train to Cry." Then he announced, "That's all," and the musicians left the stage. Further booing

8 Which is to say, Bob Dylan was, for all intents and purposes, joined onstage by the Paul Butterfield Blues Band! Bloomfield and the rhythm section had been wrangled by organist Al Kooper the day before, and three songs were rehearsed during the night. It was, apparently, not the most comfortable mix of musicians. "It was a tough night," Al Kooper has said. "Complicated and ugly."

ensued, some of it provoked by the electric nature of the set, some by the fact that the set had been only five songs long. Peter Yarrow of Peter, Paul and Mary rushed onstage to assure the crowd that Dylan would be back, that he was just fetching his acoustic guitar.[9] Behind the scenes, Joan Baez was urging Dylan to re-take the stage. He did so with some reluctance, bringing his acoustic with him. This quieted the crowd, as it seemed something of a capitulation. When he discovered he hadn't brought the right harmonica (you remember, they come in different keys), he asked if anyone had one in E. There came a clattering of oblong silver projectiles. Dylan retrieved one, fitted it into the holder, and performed "Mr. Tambourine Man" and "It's All Over Now, Baby Blue."

IT DOES seem, after all these years, to have been a lot of to-do about little. The Band's Robbie Robertson opined, "It seemed kind of a funny statement to me at the time, that somebody's gone electric. It was like, jeez, somebody's just bought a television." But I suppose the crowd could sense what was really going on: the division between the two ways in which music could be "popular" were being bound together with the violence of a welding torch. Before that, music could be "by and of the people"—socially conscious, eager to precipitate change—or it could be "enjoyed by the masses," a little bit glib and innocuous. The Beatles were not, at least not at that moment in history, interested in social change. They were, it seems to me, lyrically interested only in cataloguing the vagaries of banal relationships. In this, they were part of

9 Yarrow ostensibly supported Dylan's decision to "go electric," though he later said, "It was as if all of a sudden you saw Martin Luther King, Jr., doing a cigarette ad."

a tradition that, although it is age-old, seems to have been exacerbated by World War II. Certain songs have always been light-hearted—inconsequential—and such songs were welcomed, I'm suggesting, by a war-weary world. In 1946, for instance, the big radio hits included Bing Crosby's rendition of "Sioux City Sue" (in which the singer pledges to swap his horse and his dog for the red-haired, blue-eyed object of his affection) and "Shoo Fly Pie and Apple Pan Dowdy."

This tendency toward frivolity was still dominating the radio waves in the early sixties. Consider "Who Put the Bomp (in the Bomp, Bomp, Bomp)." The style of music in that song is "doo-wop," which tells us something right there, that there exists a genre characterized by its use of nonsense syllables. "Who Put the Bomp" was written by Gerry Goffin and Barry Mann, and is, I think, agreeably self-mocking. Still, just because one mocks oneself for doing something doesn't mean that one should have done the thing in the first place.

Here's my very unpopular stance. I think the Beatles, with their unprecedented popularity, did more than anyone else in their early days to deplete the music coming out of our radios of any remaining meaning or significance. And who came in their immediate wake? Freddie and the Dreamers. Herman's Hermits, with front man Peter Noone smugly recycling old music hall songs. There were, admittedly, groups that evidenced more substance and grit. The Animals seemed to come from a genuine place, informed by council houses, disease, and flat ale. But while you might think the blues-based Rolling Stones had more, er, balls, I remind you of the earlier quote citing the loss of meaning in the British reworkings of American blues. By 1965, with so much music sounding so similar—the twang of electric guitars, the wrecking-ball bounce of the bass, snappy snares and cymbal washes—some people feared a diminishing of music's intent and purpose.

This is what they feared, I think, when Dylan went electric.

It's also important to note that this event took place at a folk festival.[10]

Silly songs weren't the only musical response to World War II. Over in Scotland, the first Edinburgh International Festival was held in 1947 in an effort to raise post-war spirits. Finding the festival's offerings too establishment for their taste, eight little theatrical companies more or less gate-crashed the event, putting on their own shows near the officially sanctioned ones. The movement eventually became the Edinburgh Festival Fringe. In the same spirit, the Edinburgh Labour Festival Committee was created, with representation from various trade unions, significantly the Musicians Union and the Workers' Music Association.[11]

---

10 Folk festivals have the same heart beating deep within. They are egalitarian, rarely making special accommodation for the moneyed or privileged. Or the performers, for that matter. At Blue Skies, held near the town of Clarendon, Ontario, everybody camps out, which surprised some members of Porkbelly Futures. The organizers had erected our tents on the periphery of a little enclave called "The Swamp," and that night, sweating in a sleeping bag designed for penguin observation in Antarctica, I zipped the vent open for a feeble blast of air. In the morning—many of you are ahead of me here—the tent was filled with mosquitoes. Breakfast was very tasty, as were lunch and dinner, but Marty, Chas, and I felt ourselves growing weaker. It dawned on us with a sick-making thud that they were not feeding us meat. We were eating *meat substitutes*. The next day, the three of us snuck out and drove the hundred kilometres down to Kingston, where we located a Keg and devoured a cow. We tried to find a hotel, but none were available in the city, it being the August long weekend. Then a motel—but none were available, it being, you know. With great resignation, we returned to the campground and climbed into our downy sacks.

11 Which began in 1936, to quote from their website, "when five London Labour Choirs met to perform together at a time when the world was hurtling towards a struggle to contain the menace of fascism; embodied in the conflict of the Spanish Civil War; the development of the holocaust; wholesale genocide, and the suppression of human spirit."

The committee organized a People's Festival, and a man named Hamish Henderson was asked to arrange a ceilidh, a musical panoply of indigenous music. The first took place on August 31, 1951. You can listen to this ceilidh if you're so inclined, because Alan Lomax was on hand to record it. There were fiddlers and Gaelic singers, balladeers and mucklers. I am hypothesizing it was from that first People's Ceilidh that folk festivals have multiplied, steadfastly retaining their egalitarian nature. They are extensions of men like Hamish Henderson, who was a folksinger, a poet, an orator, a philosopher, a humanist, a soldier, a spy, and—I think this is extremely cool—the man to whom the Italians formally surrendered, at the end of World War II.

Folk festivals are extensions of another man who was present at that first People's Ceilidh, too. He had been present at the Edinburgh Festival as a playwright and a man of the theatre. His name at the time was James Miller. At one point, according to George Bernard Shaw, Miller was the best living playwright in Britain (other than Shaw himself). Miller was a dangerous kind of playwright; he and his first wife, Joan Littlewood, had founded the Theatre Workshop, an agitprop outfit that was once "bound over" by the police and forbidden to mount production for two years. But Jimmie Miller was increasingly attracted by folk song, the voice of the people. Like his friend and colleague Alan Lomax, he became a great collector of balladry, and—changing his name to Ewan Mac-Coll, to reflect his Scottish birthright—the composer himself of many a well-known song.

His most famous was the Grammy-winning "The First Time Ever I Saw Your Face." It was written for MacColl's third wife, Peggy Seeger, half-sister of Pete, the man who ranted and raved at Newport in 1965 and wished he had an axe with which to banish electricity. (And yes, I realize I've left out a wife. That would be dancer Jean Newlove, mother of two of MacColl's children, one of which was Kristy MacColl, the singer joining the Pogues for the rousing "Fairytale of New York.") While I've no doubt that the romantic underpinning of "The First Time Ever I Saw Your Face" was deep and heartfelt, the song was in fact written at Peggy's request. She was in the United States at the time, acting in a play, and felt the production lacked something. MacColl wrote the song very quickly and taught it to Peggy over the phone, as his Communist background prevented him from entering the USA.[12]

So it was, let me suggest, with the spirit of such men, Ewan MacColl and Hamish Henderson, looking over his shoulder that Robert Zimmerman elected to "go electric," to take folk music away from the big-P People and give it to the small-p people.[13] Or what was left of folk music, that is, because on that day in 1965, Dylan effectively made the term meaningless. Indeed, "folk music" these days is usually synonymous with "acoustic music," as though people were still trying to reject Dylan's unholy endorsement of electricity.

12 MacColl wrote the song in 1957—this is the kind of story we songwriters love—but it remained unknown for twelve years, at which point first-time film director Clint Eastwood used the song to underpin a love scene in his movie *Play Misty for Me*. Three years later, as recorded by Roberta Flack, "The First Time Ever I Saw Your Face" was awarded the Grammy for Song of the Year.

13 MacColl wrote in the September 1965 issue of *Sing Out!* magazine, "our traditional songs and ballads are the creations of extraordinarily talented artists working inside traditions formulated over time... But what of Bobby Dylan?... A youth of mediocre talent. Only a completely noncritical audience, nourished on the watery pap of pop music, could have fallen for such tenth-rate drivel."

People continued to boo at Newport after Dylan left the stage, prompting his famously acerbic comment that "they must be pretty rich to go someplace to boo." But—even though I thrilled as a boy to "Like a Rolling Stone,"[14] and have since then played music so loud my hearing is irreparably damaged—I'm not sure they were entirely wrong in doing so.

And now you know why some of my acquaintances refer to me as "Paul Quarrelsome."

---

14 One of the things I thrilled to, I should mention, was the organ, a musical squalling as insistent as eaglets wanting to be fed. It was played by Al Kooper, although he had originally gone to that session to play guitar. There was this other guy there, Mike Bloomfield. Kooper listened to him warm up, then rather sheepishly re-cased his own instrument and turned his attention to the keyboards.

[5]

Here is how I would spend some Saturday nights when I was a teenager.

The first thing you need to understand is that there were many, many Saturday nights when I had nothing to do. I am not trying to claim any special sense of isolation or loneliness. That's the state of existence for all teenagers: nothing to do. Teenagers today, despite the mind-boggling advances made by science and technology, still have nothing to do. They have more ways to occupy themselves whilst they do nothing, that's all. All I had was television and, well, a little dink-twiddling from time to time.

But I hated having nothing to do on Saturday nights, and I still do. Any other night of the week, and I'm perfectly content with my own company. Even Friday, when the workaday lads are pounding the city's fun button, I have no problem staying at home and keeping my own counsel. But Saturdays, I am compelled to shore up my small puddles of energy against the ever-constant lassitude and hit the streets.

In my youth, these Saturday evenings would begin with, of all things, a consideration of wardrobe. Now, it's true, one of the benefits of being a bluesman from Don Mills, Ontario, is that you don't have to think much about the clothes you wear. Indeed, if you do, you aren't really a bluesman. I usually wore jeans and t-shirts, some kind of boot to account for my splay-footed waddle. But these Saturday nights, I would try to dress myself with style, which usually involved a madras shirt with a "matching" dickie. I'm not sure if you remember dickies, which were turtlenecks. Not turtleneck *sweaters*, understand, just the actual turtleneck, with enough material down the front and back so that someone might believe that, beneath your shirt, you wore the full garment—or they might believe it if they had spectacularly bad eyesight and a double-digit IQ. "Matching" is in quotes because my colour sense was a little suspect. I might also wear Beatle boots, which forced my fat toes into arrowheads with all the merciless bone-breaking of Chinese foot-binding. As for pants, I will spare you. Suffice it to say that the salient factor was tightness. Yeah.

Thus attired, I would leave the house. I was not married back then, of course; there was no one to look at me with disdain tinged with disbelief and demand, "You're not going outside like that, are you?" So I would leave, unchallenged, and I would walk out to Lawrence Avenue and wait for the eastbound bus.

A *west*bound bus would have taken me downtown. I bet you assumed that's where I was going, didn't you, to the big city. Even though Toronto was still called "Toronto the Good" by many people (chiefly Montrealers), there were some lively places. There was Yonge Street, for example, which back then had developed a truly awesome seediness. It's hard to believe that any major city, let alone Toronto, would have allowed its main commercial thoroughfare to become such a crippled stroll, the boulevard lined with strip clubs and massage parlours. And, of course, there was Yorkville, which was our version of Greenwich Village or Haight-Ashbury. I would go there, on occasion, because there were girls in Yorkville, young women with long hair and see-through blouses. The famous club the Riverboat was not licensed, which meant I could enter and see such notables as Phil Ochs,[1] Sonny Terry, and Brownie McGhee.[2] Kotzma and I spent one notable week attending the nightly performances of the Siegel-Schwall Band, an outfit from Chicago that was, in some senses, Butterfield Lite.[3] Corky Siegel and Jim Schwall met while studying at Roosevelt University. Schwall, a guitar player, came from a country music background, while Siegel (who studied saxophone, but focussed on the harmonica) favoured the blues. Their sound resulted from an attempt to combine these two genres, which I suppose explains why I liked them so

1   The most overtly political and active of the "protest singers," Ochs was a good friend of Bob Dylan's until a famous incident in which Phil's criticism of one of Bob's songs prompted the latter to throw the former out of his limousine, proclaiming, "You're not a folk singer, you're a journalist!" Mentally unstable and increasingly alcoholic, Ochs wandered the world, at one point meeting and singing with Victor Jara. Ochs was so upset by Jara's death during the 1973 *coup d'etat* in Chile that he organized a huge benefit at Madison Square Garden. Pete Seeger and Arlo Guthrie were scheduled to play. When it looked as if sluggish ticket sales would force them to cancel the event, Dylan agreed to perform, and the evening was sold out.

2   Sonny Terry and Brownie McGhee were a duo (Terry played harmonica and McGhee guitar) who were among Alan Lomax's discoveries. What I think is most interesting about them is, by the time they were playing the Riverboat in Toronto the two men could no longer stand each other. But they were bound together by symbiosis: McGhee, who had suffered from polio as a child, needed to be pushed around in a wheelchair. Terry, the wheeler, was blind and needed to be told where to go.

3   Indeed, the Siegel-Schwall Band took over the house-band gig at Big John's when Butterfield and the boys began touring.

much. In many ways this is what we tried to do, years later, with Porkbelly Futures. But I'm getting ahead of myself. That's not the point of this aside, anyway; I was concerned rather with delivering a memory. There's Kotzma and me attending every night of a week-long stint, sitting as close as we could to the Siegel-Schwall Band, who knew us as the kids who came to see every show. As they played the blues, Corky Siegel would wail on his harp (remember your terminology, now), drawing in and flattening his thirds and sevenths with very deep-throated howls. Every so often (actually, quite often, compared to other harpists) a reed would snap inside the harmonica. Corky Siegel would reach for a fresh instrument with one hand, and with the other pass the busted harp to Kotzma.

But I rarely ventured down to Yorkville on my own. As mentioned above, there were young women with long hair and see-through blouses there, but don't forget I was wearing a dickie and a madras shirt. So I would board the eastbound bus, which took me into the wilds of Scarborough.

I've mentioned Scarborough before. Patrick Murphy, the Manure bassist, came from there, and, as noted, it was a slightly better place for a bluesman to be from than Don Mills. My high school actually serviced both Don Mills and Scarborough, abutting as it did the divisional road, Victoria Park Avenue. It was a cruel and damnable stereotype (but like all such cruel and damnable stereotypes, not without foundation) that a lad from Don Mills would be enrolled in a five-year academic program while a Scarborough boy would register in four-year tech. There were even *two*-year tech guys, gormless fellows with tattoos and decks of smokes folded into the sleeves of their t-shirts. They took apart cars and put them back together again, biding time until their sixteenth birth-days. And while I could not in fairness claim that all of these guys came from Scarborough, I would bet a lot of money that none of them were from Don Mills.

If you have an interest in the biographies of musicians, this might all have a familiar ring. The young white lad, eager to immerse himself in the blues, travels out of suburbia and ven-tures into the black ghettoes. That's not what's going on here. I like to think I would have done that. I mean, I did what I could, buying recordings of performers like Charley Patton and Blind Lemon Jefferson and Robert Johnson. I didn't like them much, but I bought them.[4] And when opportunity presented itself I would hurry out to hear performances given by Albert King and Buddy Guy. (The former performed at Toronto's Massey Hall, the latter at the aforementioned Riverboat. Buddy Guy, using the advanced technology of cordless radio transmission, would leave the club and play out on the side-walk of bustling Yorkville Avenue, shilling for his own show.) But the biggest obstacle to my adhering to the template men-tioned above was that Toronto, in those days, lacked a sizable black community. No, in heading into the heart of Scarbor-ough, I was seeking out the white working class. Scarborough was peopled with hard-drinking people—in my imagination, the men are uniformly gnome-like and wear grog-blossomed noses, the women are large and lack teeth—of various descent, although I would say the largest demographic was Scottish. I

4   In a previous chapter I mentioned Charley Patton's famous Grafton, Wisconsin, ses-sions of 1930. What isn't always mentioned about Patton is that you can barely under-stand anything the man is saying. This is not simply a function of archaic recording techniques. He was a mumbler, more concentrated on whacking his guitar in an admittedly very funky manner. (Not all the time, only when the spirit overtook him.) What I'm getting at is, it was not the most satisfying listening experience.

can't cite statistics, but I can tell you that my destination (I descended the bus at Kennedy Avenue) was a curling rink, the Broom & Stone. On Saturday evenings, back in the late sixties, the curlers were forced to retire to the club room, and the sheets were given over to soul music.

THERE WERE four stages set up on the cardinal points of the ice (I guess there was some covering over the ice; at least, I don't remember the dancers going down all the time), and the audience would move, herdlike, to assemble in front of the active one. Each stage contained more or less the same equipment. Traynor amplifiers constituted the backline.[5] Off to one side sat a couple of hulking wooden crates: one, a Hammond B-3 electric organ, the other, a Leslie cabinet.[6] Five young men would take to the stage. I suppose there might have been some quartets, or sextets, but they were uncommon. Invariably, the configuration was bass, drums, guitar, organ, and lead singer. They were dressed identically. That is, the members of each quintet were dressed identically. They took pains not to be dressed the same as, or even similarly to, any of the other quintets. That is why some of the groups were dressed even worse than myself, as though they were attending some Formal Event for the Criminally Insane. Pinstripes were common, and satiny sheens. The singer was allowed a little latitude. Sometimes he wore a different suit from the others

---

5   Traynor amplifers were, of all things, manufactured by a wholly Canadian company, a rare example of frostbacks actually thinking they could do something as well as, maybe even better than, the Americans.

6   If I give the cabinet its full name—and you really think about it—you might understand what it is I'm talking about: the Leslie Rotating Tremolo Speaker System. It's a sound modification device (as opposed to a mere amplifier) that takes the organ sound and spins it around in the air like *boleadoras*.

(the same cut, mind you, with the material a complementary colour, or an attempt at such), and he was allowed to strip down a bit, to remove the jacket and loosen the tie. Often this stripping down happened as the set progressed. The singer, after all, would be engaged in some pretty strenuous activity, his fists clenched in rapture, light streaks shooting off his patent-leather shoes, his eyes focussed on some Gloryland far away. As I remember it, the singers for the first three groups would introduce songs by saying things like, "I was talking to my friend George the other day..." or "This is a song I learned from my friend George..."

It took a couple of hours to make the circuit of all four stages. By the time we arrived at the last one, the crowd was jittery with anticipation. We emitted a low rumble, like an idling '56 Bel Air. When a voice announced the next group—the Mandala!—there was an eruption that registered on the Richter.

You know who was in that group?

George.

George Olliver would glide sideways to the centre of the stage, carried there by a vacillation of his right heel and toe that was so small as to be virtually undetectable. At any rate, a lot of George's foot action was shrouded by the bell of his bell-bottoms. He would snatch the microphone out of its clip with an irritated, almost violent motion, as though he'd been looking for it all day long and this was the last place he expected to find it. He held the mic in an overly fussy way, his hand curled upwards, fingers often pointing outwards in a nancy manner.

"I've come four thousand miles," he'd bark at the crowd. "Maybe here I can find my opportunity..."

And the band would kick in with the rhythm, which I am producing even as I write this, my cheeks puffed and my lips slapping together explosively.

"People have always made a fool of me..."

George's voice possessed a high huskiness. His diction was clipped and his vowels tight. The lines he produced were embellished with bluesy glissandos and grace notes. And when the guitarist stepped forward to solo,[7] George would throw the microphone back into the clip, glide sideways and begin to dance. This he would do with a degree of muscularity, his dancing being comparable, as I recall it now, to the figure skating of Elvis Stojko. Indeed, the two men share a distinctive physiology, their limbs ever so slightly truncated. Many of their moves have a pugnacious quality, as though the two men were card-carrying members of the Lollipop Guild. And often, wee moments before the instrumental interlude ended, George would drop into the splits. He would pause there a moment, sucking in air greedily, and then squeeze his legs together, propelling himself heavenward. He'd grab at the mic again and launch into the new verse.

Just so we're clear on this point: George was white. All of the singers and all of the musicians were white. True, they were following the lead of the Mandala, playing R&B: "Knock On Wood," "Hold On, I'm Coming," "Soul Man," etcetera. But in Toronto, back in the late sixties, black musicians were a rarity, treated with the same kind of wonder and curiosity that Londoners a century previous evinced toward Jemmy Button, who had been transported there from his native

---

7 I want to point out that I use the phrase "step forward" only figuratively. The guitarist would actually remain in the shadows, studying his hands with the intensity of a Talmudic scholar.

Tierra del Fuego aboard the *Beagle* (with Charles Darwin riding shotgun).

England had a much more inviting immigration policy in the fifties and sixties than did Canada, trying to recover after World War ii. Then, when England decided that things had recovered as best they could, it played kitty-bar-the-door. The governments of many Caribbean countries began to pressure Canada to rescind the "climate unsuitability" clause in our immigration policy. When they were successful, thousands of new people arrived in Ottawa, Montreal, and Toronto.

But before this happened, Toronto, as I've said, lacked a sizable black community. Not that the city was all that homogenous. For example, the members of the Mandala, in addition to George, were Don Elliot (bass); Pentti (Whitey) Glan (drums); Josef Chirowski (big hulking b-3); and Domenic Troiano (guitar). Their names indicated a typically Torontonian admixture of heritage: Anglo, Finnish, German, and Italian. When I wasn't watching George—and it was a little hard to take one's eyes off him—I was concentrating on Dom Troiano.

I haven't mentioned it yet, but by this time I had gained a reputation as a hotshot young guitarist. I owned an Epiphone Broadway guitar—a thick, black, jazz-styled electric—and I had an old tube amplifier. The combination produced a satisfyingly thick wail, feedback lashing out like a lion's paw through the cage's bars. I was fast, too, and there were some little tricks I could do, *memes*, triplet figures that could be easily moved up and down the fretboard. So some people thought I was a hotshot. True, all of these people were young men who smoked way too much dope. (It pains me to point out that there were no girls who thought I was a hotshot.)

But I knew I wasn't really all that good. I knew that my brain lagged far behind my fat little fingers, that I didn't really understand music and its complexities. I knew, for example, that I would never be able to play like Dom Troiano. If the two of us stood on a stage together and played, I realized, the difference would be obvious. I would be grappling with my big Epiphone, wringing its neck and plucking notes out of its belly. Troiano would be coaxing the music out of his guitar— significantly, a Fender Stratocaster[8]—caressing the thing gently and producing high wails, the kind of sounds I imagined a beautiful woman would make on the brink of orgasm.

When Dom Troiano soloed on the song "Opportunity," he opened with a squalling insistence, a repeated, bluesy, and very elastic interval. From there he would venture higher and higher on the fretboard, until it seemed that there were no longer any actual notes, just emotion and wild-eyed freedom.

ALLOW ME to flash ahead in time for a moment here. Don Elliot was involved in a serious car accident in 1968, forcing

---

8 Why, you might ask, did I attach the word "significantly" to the Fender Stratocaster? (You might also ask why I used such a heavy-handed and sophomoric analogy, but let's gloss over that for now and talk about guitars.) The significance has to do with the musicological thesis that I'm about to promote.

Ahem.

The Fender guitar was significant to the development of the Toronto Sound.

There is indeed a Toronto Sound, and as far as I'm concerned, it is as distinct as anything coming out of Philadelphia, Detroit, Chicago, or New Orleans. David Clayton Thomas, frontman for the band Blood, Sweat and Tears, was one of its early proponents. Listen to him singing "You've Made Me So Very Happy," if you care to; that's the Toronto Sound. I characterize it as Sweet Soul Music, with the sweetness purely musical in nature. The sweetness has to do with a major tonality, unflattened thirds and L.A. fifths abounding. Also featured prominently in the Toronto Sound is a Hammond B-3. With Leslies. Toronto has produced a statistically unlikely number of wonderful organists: Joey Chirowski, Mike Fonfara, Doug Riley, Richard Bell.

him to leave the group. Josef Chirowski established himself with the group Crowbar, where he replaced keyboardist Richard Bell, later of Porkbelly Futures. Whitey Glan had a very successful career and managed to make his way south of the border; he played with people like Alice Cooper and Lou Reed. Glan and Dom Troiano also had success with the group Bush, their best-known song being the energetic and emphatic "I Can Hear You Calling." Troiano was diagnosed with prostate cancer in the 1990s and struggled with it for ten years before passing away. "Struggled with it," "lived with it," I'm not sure what the most appropriate phrase is. And I certainly don't know why the gods act with such offhandedness, flicking their fingers with irritation as they allow some to ascend, others to plummet to their doom.

But back at the Broom & Stone, these beautiful young men were in their prime, with only promise ahead. Dom Troiano was finishing his solo in "Opportunity," his final notes suspended somewhere in the Kuiper belt. George continued dancing, pulling angrily at his collar and shirt buttons.

George Olliver was the Blue-Eyed Prince of Soul, praying at the altar of James Brown. Like Brown, Olliver was in part a hopped-up preacher man, his invocations just this side of speaking in tongues—or complete gibberish, depending on where you locate the Holy Ghost in all this. George led the audience through the Five Steps to Soul, which eschewed doctrine and coherency and promised that salvation was to be had in music.

George Olliver still performs, and he still performs Sweet Soul Music, although he now has a split focus. As a born-again Christian, George sings gospel whenever and wherever he can, serving the ministry of Jesus Christ. I may not be a born-again Christian, but I can certainly see the appeal in singing gospel.

The connection between blues and gospel music has been proclaimed by more eloquent and authentic voices than mine. "The blues is a lot like Church," said Lightnin' Hopkins. "When a preacher's up there preaching the Bible, he's honest to God tryin' to get you to understand these things. Well, singing the blues is the same thing." Blues and gospel share the same unbridling of the spirit, in which the singer shakes off the constraints of propriety, just as James Brown would shake off the cape his handlers wrapped around his shoulders in an attempt to get him quieted down, sedated, moved off the stage.

Blues and gospel are flip sides of the same musical coin— songs of complaint, songs of belief—with that coin most definitely tossed by an African-American hand. Oh, there is gospel that white people create, but to me it doesn't sound remotely similar. Songs such as "Shall We Gather at the River?" and "The Church in the Wildwood" are dreary and dirge-like. Their melodies—typically sung in unison rather than in harmony—have creepy rises and falls that remind me of Druids gathered in the palest of moonlight. But I will say this: "Church in the Wildwood" comes with a pretty good story attached to it. Dr. William Pitts, in the year of Our Lord 1857, was travelling by stagecoach out of his native Wisconsin to meet his fiancée. The stagecoach stopped for a bit in Bradford, Iowa, and Pitts took a little walk. He came upon a glade, a "setting of rare beauty," as he put it, and he imagined he saw a church, a humble brown church, sitting there. It was an image he could not shake, and when he returned home, he wrote a song about it. Happenstance had it that William Pitts moved to Bradford seven years later, to teach music at the local academy. He was stunned to find the townspeople in the act of erecting a church on the very spot of his intense imaginings. He had his students sing the song at the opening, and he subsequently sold the rights to a music publisher for twenty-five dollars, money he needed to attend medical school. The song is still sung, and the little brown church still stands today.

Let us compare this quaint little tale to the story of the man often cited as the Father of Black Gospel,[9] Thomas A. Dorsey.

Under another name, "Georgia Tom," Dorsey and the similarly monikered Tampa Red (Hudson Whittaker) constituted a duet called the Hokum Boys. Georgia Tom played the piano, Tampa Red a big-bodied steel guitar in the bottleneck style. "Hokum" is characterized by sexual content and a heavy reliance on the double entendre. It was in that tradition that Thomas A. Dorsey made his debut in taverns and tiny theatres across the USA. Their hit record of 1928, "It's Tight Like That," is a hokum exemplar if ever there was one:

> Two old ladies waiting in the sand,
> Each one wishing that the other was a man,
> It's tight like that...

But Tragedy entered the scene—the gods waggled their fingers—when Georgia Tom's wife died in childbirth. Heartbroken, he turned to the Lord, and in his grief came to him his

---

9 I've been confused for years about the difference between a gospel song and a "spiritual." I'm not absolutely convinced there is one, but I did read, in a book by Studs Terkel, that a spiritual is a song that arose from the slave days, in the folk tradition, and is not attributed to any composer. A gospel song is authored, and Thomas Dorsey was one of the first to write one.

most famous song, "Take My Hand, Precious Lord." Dorsey's influence on gospel music goes beyond imbuing it with the rhythms and airs of the blues and hokum. He also wrote highly subjective lyrics—"I'm tired, I'm weak, I'm lone"—a subtle shift from the congregation to the individual. "Take My Hand, Precious Lord" was sung at a rally the evening before Rev. Martin Luther King's assassination and was sadly reprised, by Mahalia Jackson, at his funeral. Lyndon B. Johnson left instructions that "Take My Hand, Precious Lord" be sung at his own funeral. The song has been recorded by many of gospel's stars and, interestingly enough, by many stars of country and western music, including Roy Rogers and Tennessee Ernie Ford. Why is that interesting? Well, consider this: Thomas A. Dorsey was the first African-American to be inducted into the Nashville Songwriters Hall of Fame. Given that that institution was probably the last bastion of white musical exclusivity, I think it's interesting that integration came in the form of gospel music.

This line of investigation will take us to some interesting places, including Nashville itself. But please bear with me—it is much too early in the story to go there yet.

CHAPTER

[6]

Remember DR. Hill's son, Danny? (He had come to audition for PQ's People and sampled some strange Sinatra stuff; he didn't get the job.) Well, the year I was sixteen, one of my high school music teachers came up to me and said that the organizers would like an original song for the upcoming Christmas assembly. "Hmm," I said, "I guess I could do that."[1]

"Great," she said. (My memory being what it is, I can't be 100 per cent sure, but I'm thinking this was Miss Sage, who taught strings and had long blonde hair and broke my heart

---

[1] I don't think I would be so glib today. After all, if we disregard the huge and nebulous thing called "love"—hey, there's a song title!—there are probably more songs written about Christmas than about anything else. An enduring Christmas song is the Holy Grail for songwriters. For example, aside from all his other talents and accomplishments, Mel Tormé's most lucrative artistic achievement was no doubt co-writing "The Christmas Song (Chestnuts Roasting on an Open Fire)." It is akin to winning the lottery, writing a popular Yuletide ditty, and subject to the same whimsical winds of fate. Take the music teacher, Don Gardner, who noticed that his charges, seven- and eight-year-old children, could not say certain words without issuing little whistling sounds. He went home and wrote "All I Want for Christmas Is My Two Front Teeth."

by marrying one of the other music teachers before I had a chance to fully mature.) "I've asked Danny Hill, too. You guys can write it together."

"Oh." During the first few seconds of our conversation, I had already vaulted ahead in my imagination. I was projecting mere months into the future, by which time this triumph—the first public performance of a new Christmas classic—had led to my performance at the Mariposa Folk Festival, where the entire audience was composed of women who had removed their blouses in deference to the sun and its heat. Now this Danny guy had come along to scupper the deal. But I went over to his house anyway, toting my Goya, the fairly cheap acoustic guitar that I'd managed to acquire.[2]

We went down into the basement, and Danny picked up his own guitar, which was a nylon-stringed instrument. This was a bit odd and unexampled. To my mind, nylon strings were used to play classical music and had very few, um, *practical* applications. Dan had also grown out the nails on his right hand, and with these effeminate extensions he plucked at his guitar, arpeggiating. (In those days, I would strum. I was beginning to experiment with Travis picking, but I had never seen anyone do this, the picking hand hovering over the strings. Everything the kid did was strange.) "I've been working on the song," Danny announced. "Want to hear what I have so far?"

---

2 I had a paper route for many years as a boy, which required a weekly collection of monies. One of my customers was Lloyd Percival, the great hockey genius. Great hockey genius, perhaps, but too often not at home. Even when he was home, Percival usually claimed to have no cash, that such matters were the purview of his wife, although there was never any evidence of such a creature. Anyway, one afternoon I found the universe in perfect harmony. Lloyd was at home, his wallet was stuffed, he agreed to pay up. Thus I believe was my guitar acquired.

"Sure."

"Okay, listen." He ramped up his spirited little arpeggiating. *"Christmas comes once a year, now's the time to be of good cheer."* He continued in this jaunty vein, rhyming words colliding with each other like bumper cars. I didn't know what to think. This was really terrible, this whole enterprise was doomed to—

Then Danny burst out laughing. He pointed at my face, whooping with delight, and after a few seconds, just as I was about to join in, he stopped abruptly and said, "Okay. Let's get to work."

Well, we did in fact write a Christmas song, of which I can remember very little. Years later Danny reminded me that we had argued over which phrase was correct: "giving and taking was a beautiful thing" or "giving and taking were a beautiful thing." I can't remember if "giving and taking were beautiful things" was in the running, but it clearly should have been. At any rate, our song was a big success at the Christmas assembly, and even though there was no A&R (Artist and Repertoire) guy from a major label ready to sign us to a big contract, we decided to form a duet, which we called Quarrington Hill, just as Martin and I would later form Quarrington/Worthy. This doesn't represent any egotism on my part—or, let's say it doesn't *reveal* the egotism we all know to be there—since Quarrington is a bulky name and would sit oddly on the other side of the couplings.

Danny (he achieved fame as Dan, of course, and what I call him is Dan-Dan) and I wrote a few songs together, and we both penned a couple of originals. (Again, gone from the memory banks.) Quarrington Hill also did a couple of covers, one of which I *can* remember, "Father and Son" by Cat

Stevens. This song is a dialogue, with Stevens singing the older man's part in a lower register and going up an octave to portray the rebellious offspring. I would sing the father's role, and then Dan-Dan would come in and carve my ass in a beautiful silver voice tarnished by painful emotion. In terms of making *me* look good, this song was a misguided venture, but it always went over very well. Not that Quarrington Hill played that many places. We did manage to convince a bar on Jarvis Street (never the most wholesome avenue in Toronto the Good) to let us play nightly, and after dinner I would borrow my father's car, drive over to pick up Dan-Dan, and drive downtown. This arrangement lasted a week or so before the owner asked Dan-Dan how old we were. "Seventeen and sixteen," he replied blithely.

"Butbutbut," the owner stammered, "this is a *bar.*"

"Oh."

Danny was much more ambitious than I, and a much more talented performer, and after a few months Quarrington Hill ceased to be. Quarrington went back to the basement, and Hill became a very famous Canadian songwriter. He achieved international fame as the singer and co-writer of "Sometimes When We Touch," a song that, while some may find it overly earnest, packs an enormous emotional wallop. Dan had first written the words to "Sometimes" at age nineteen, along with a chord structure and a melody that are lost to oblivion. This is perhaps the neatest and clearest form of collaboration, one party handling the music, the other the lyrics.

LIKE GEORGE Gershwin and his brother Ira.

The Gershvins, having emigrated to New York from Russia, decided that their bookish and bespectacled older boy, Izzy,[3] should have music lessons, so they bought a piano and had it installed in their second-floor walk-up. Before Izzy could lay a finger on the instrument, his little brother Jacob came running into the room and, kind of miraculously, pounded out a passable version of a current popular song. (He had learned to play, it is said, by staring for hours at a friend's player piano.) Ira went back to his books, and Jacob—who called himself George—went on to demonstrate a fierce brand of musical genius. He was interested in all sorts of music, from popular song to classical European stuff to the avant-garde.[4] At the age of fifteen, George got a job as a song plugger down on Tin Pan Alley. This was an area of Manhattan, mostly on West 28th Street between 5th and 6th avenues, where there was a concentration of sheet music publishers. Tin Pan Alley blossomed in the last half of the nineteenth century, before the coming of the radio and the phonograph, when musical entertainment at home meant sitting down at the piano and doing it yourself. The odd name of the place supposedly stems from the fact that there were hundreds of tinkling pianos sounding in dissonance. George's first hit— "When You Want 'Em, You Can't Get 'Em, When You've Got 'Em, You Don't Want 'Em"—violated a basic Tin Pan Alley dictate, which was to keep the title short.

Ira worked in his father's Turkish baths and continued to read his books. But George Gershwin—once he changed from "Gershvin" to "Gershwin," the entire family followed

3   He was called "Izzy" from birth, and by the time he got around to wondering what his real name was, his parents had forgotten. He thenceforth assumed it was Isadore—it was, in fact, Israel—but he settled the issue by going with Ira.

4   I will ignore—it's outside the scope of my little book—the miracle of George's excursions into the realm of "serious" music with his creation of such marvels as *Rhapsody in Blue*, still a staple in the concert hall.

suit—called upon his brother for help when he began writing for the musical theatre. The boys took their show to Broadway.

George usually came up with the music first, at least, the initial musical seed. Ira laboured long and hard over the text. He would sometimes stay awake all night, struggling to find just the perfect word. The music to what would become "Embraceable You" so daunted him that he had to check into a hotel for three days to work out the lyrics.

Another famous site of collaboration was the Brill Building, located at 1619 Broadway Avenue, with its offices leased to music publishers, composers, arrangers, and recording engineers. Musicians loitered around the lobby, hoping to be hired to play for a demo. That was the actual Brill Building, but when people use the term they are mostly referring to a neighbouring building at 1650. This is where Aldon Music kept its offices, and it was Aldon Music (run by Don Kirshner and Al Nevins) that had the most successful stable of songwriting teams, none of its creators older than twenty-six years of age: Neil Sedaka and Howard Greenfield; Doc Pomus and Mort Shuman; Gerry Goffin and Carole King; Tommy Boyce and Bobby Hart; Barry Mann and Cynthia Weil.

Arguably the most influential was the team of Leiber & Stoller (Jerry and Mike, respectively), who pioneered a lot of revolutionary ideas we now perceive as commonplace. They incorporated teenage slang into popular music ("Yakety Yak"), championed "girl groups" like the Shangri-Las, and, as producers, used orchestration, strings, and such to enhance rhythm and blues. In doing so, they influenced a weird kid who liked to hang around the place, Phil Spector.[5]

Great songwriting teams are book-worthy subject matter all on their own, so I'm going to limit myself here to things you might find interesting. (Which is to say, I suspect you might not know these things, so you have to suffer through this pon- · cey delivery of the fruits of my research.) For instance: Gerry Goffin and Carole King were a married couple, responsible for many songs identified strongly with a female mindset: "(You Make Me Feel Like) A Natural Woman," for one, and "Will You Love Me Tomorrow." But King supplied the music to these co-compositions, and it was Goffin who supplied the lyrics. Carole King, as you know, went on to find great success as a solo performer. Her album *Tapestry* was one of the best-selling LPs of all time. You remember *Tapestry*, don't you? It was the album that everyone's girlfriend liked.

There was another very successful married-couple/writing team; indeed, they met at 1650 Broadway Avenue. Barry Mann had already written or co-written some hit songs[6] by the time he met Cynthia Weil, an aspiring actress. Together they wrote such classics as "We Gotta Get out of This Place" and "You've Lost That Lovin' Feelin'."

And this brings us back to Dan Hill, because Dan-Dan's collaborator (the first was Paul-Paul Quarrington) was Barry Mann. Dan went to meet Mann at the Motown Building in Hollywoodland, California. (The building housed the L.A. offices of ATV music, which had signed both men.) They

5 Here's something not many people know: on the original recording of "On Broadway," performed by the Drifters in 1963, the guitar that can be heard squalling away in echo-land is played by Phil Spector. I've another little suchlike tidbit. Leiber & Stoller were also responsible for Peggy Lee's hit "Is That All There Is?" The tune's orchestration was unlike anything heard on radio at the time. It is large, capricious, emotive, as though written to accompany a movie filmed in Technicolor. The parts were scored and conducted by a very young Randy Newman.

6 Including "Who Put the Bomp." Apparently Mann can be a little bristly, feeling that he has never gotten the credit he's due, and from time to time bemoans the fact that he never had a big hit under his own name. Except he did: "Who Put the Bomp?"

exchanged ideas. Or rather, Barry Mann fired off a number of musical ideas, inveighing young Dan to provide lyrics, something Danny found himself curiously unable to do. As Dan-Dan reports, "I still clung to the clichéd notion that songwriting could only come from a pure, inspired place." With a degree of desperation, Danny removed a sheet of lyrics from the bottom of his guitar case, instructed Mann to do something with them if he wanted, and elevated down to the reception area to call for a cab.

Before the cab arrived, Barry Mann came exploding through the elevator doors. "I got the chorus!" he yelled as he ran, singing the melody that would propel the song "Sometimes When We Touch" to number three on the *Billboard* Hot 100.

We will return to Dan Hill later in the story. Before we leave him here, however, I'm going to recount a little anecdote that is non-musical in nature, and out of order in the narrative sense. After my musical career (which you will read about in the upcoming chapters) didn't amount to much, I decided that I'd concentrate on my novel writing. I supported myself with a series of bad jobs. I believe I've already mentioned "tractor-tire stacker." I was also a dishwasher, a paralegal attaché (that's a messenger who delivers legal materials), and a security guard for the aptly named Cavalier Security company. My uniform consisted of grey slacks and a bright red jacket adorned with a crest surmounted by the word "Cavalier." I also had a hat, which was too big. (If you knew how big my head is, you'd wonder who the prototypical Cavalier man was.) The reason my hat didn't settle over my eyes and blind me was that I wore, after the fashion of the day, spectacles with lenses as large as side plates. None of my careers—in security, law, sanitation, or machinery—earned me much money. It was barely enough to cover my basic expenses, beer and smokes. So I had to cut back on a few things, namely food and rent. The food problem I solved by subsisting on a diet of Kraft Dinner. As for accommodation, I moved into the basement of my richest friend, who was, by a long shot, Dan-Dan Hill.

With the money from his hits, and barely out of his teens, Dan had bought a house in the Beaches, an old and fashionable neighbourhood in East Toronto that abuts Lake Ontario. Notice I didn't say, "Dan put a down payment on a house." No, he bought the damn thing. So for a while I lived in his basement.

The house was the location of some fairly wild parties, though not so much during the time I lived there. Dan had married a beautiful lawyer, Beverly Chapin, and the place was reasonably quiet, except for me stumbling down the stairs at three o'clock in the morning, pissed as a newt.

Late one afternoon, I returned home from work resplendent in my Cavalier Security uniform. I entered the house through the back door, picked up a glass of water in the kitchen, and, drawn by some voices, went into the living room. Bev was sitting there with a friend. Quite an attractive friend, so, without being invited, I sat down on a small chair, folded my arms, and waited to be introduced.

Bev didn't pause in her story to introduce me. Indeed, she kind of ignored me, but that was all right, I had time. Bev's friend threw me a quizzical glance, and then another. As the quizzical glances came faster and faster, Bev continued speaking in a measured manner. Finally, she left off her story long enough to announce, "Oh, that's the security guard Dan hires when he's out of town to make sure I don't fool around on him."

AFTER HIGH school, I began attending the University of Toronto, studying English Literature. I was interested in becoming a writer by then, but it quickly dawned upon me that this wasn't the way to do it. Back then there was not the proliferation of writing programs we have today (I myself have long been associated with the fine Humber School for Writers), and although I might have considered attending the Writers' Workshop at the University of Iowa, that would have required my first hearing of it. What I did do was ignore my studies to a certain degree, and at night I would bang away on an old typewriter and try to work though certain technical problems.

My childhood friend Stephen Tulk, who was in a pre-med program, took an English Literature class with me. The concentration was on the American novel, and that course was the only one that ever did anything toward equipping me to become a novelist. Specifically, Professor Asals spent two whole hours discussing the beginning of Melville's *Moby Dick*, with its famous three words, "Call me Ishmael." His lecture gave me an inkling of the depths that were possible, the vast spaces beneath words, and if that didn't teach me about writing per se, it taught me a little bit about reading. Tulk annoyed me, because when called upon by the prof he would stand and put forth an eloquent argument in defence of or opposition to a statement, despite having *never read the novel in question*. I myself was forever mired in bullshit. I remember suggesting that Captain Ahab, fearing that he would die by rope, preferred to stay at sea because it eliminated the possibility of hanging. "But one can be hanged at sea," replied the professor. "And if you'd read *Billy Budd* as you were supposed to, you would know that."

Tulk was and remains the most talented man I know. He is a fine artist and a skilled musician, as well as being a doctor. As much younger men we goofed around on musical instruments together, and Tulkie claims still to have a reel-to-reel tape recording of yours truly singing "Long Tall Texan" before my voice changed. At any rate, Tulk was a member of a musical group called the System, and one day he reported (after a class on *Pierre: or, The Ambiguities*) that his friend Martin Worthy had returned to Toronto. I remembered Martin, he of Marty's Martians and the scoliosis. "Where's he been?" I wondered.

"He's been in Europe, playing guitar and singing. You guys should get together."

I should make it plain here that I was no longer a blues guy. At the age of seventeen, I had been drawn to the Mariposa Folk Festival, held then on Toronto's Centre Island[7] because of the participation of Taj Mahal, one of my blues heroes. His band included Jesse Edwin Davis, who played the Fender Telecaster unlike anyone before or since, his work at once delicate and as forceful as a church organ. I still remember attending the workshops that featured Taj Mahal, watching the evening concert as his band took a huge crowd through the gloaming into night. But something else had happened to me there. There were these "singer-songwriters" hanging around. I remember two in particular: a scrawny and bespectacled kid named Bruce Cockburn, and James Taylor. I had never heard of James Taylor—neither, certainly, had any of my

7 I currently live on Toronto's island archipelago; at least, I spend much of the summer there, living on a houseboat.

friends—but for some reason I elected to attend his first performance at the festival, which was part of an afternoon event.

It is quite something to watch five hundred women fall in love with a guy all at the same time. And, times being what they were, many of these women had shed clothing beneath the summer sun. (This accounts for the fantasy cited at the beginning of this chapter, in reference to the Christmas song.) A few were topless, which was dizzying. I returned from the Island with a new respect for folk music and promptly became a singer-songwriter.

So, after classes one day, I took my guitar, the Goya, over to a rooming house in the Annex. Marty and his girlfriend, Jill, had a room on the second floor. That was pretty cool, to have a girlfriend, not to mention one who resided in the same tiny little bedsit. And not only that (I met her a few hours later), but also one who was vivacious and beautiful and British. Martin had met Jill in Brussels, where she had been working as an *au pair*. He himself had been working with his friend Dave Chalmers as a musical duet. They had a job in a restaurant there—that is, they were permitted to play in the restaurant and then pass around a breadbasket into which the patrons could place alms. Now Marty had returned to Toronto—I realize I don't actually know why; I'll have to ask him sometime—and was looking about for something to do. So I went over there, and Marty and I exchanged songs, and we decided that we complemented each other in many ways. One very basic way was that our voices blended nicely, my baritone and his tenor. But there were other things, too, that were less evident. Martin's lyrics were more complex, clever, poetically crafted than mine. His tonality was different—that is, his collection of musical memes. He liked, for example, to play a chord and then, retaining the rooting bass note, slide the triad up a whole tone. On this occasion (or possibly a slightly later one) we wrote a song together, then went out and drank far too much beer, a pattern we would repeat with minor variations for a long time.

Marty and I conducted our partnership in a very business-like manner. There weren't too many corporate types who would have recognized our manner as businesslike, perhaps, but I believe it set a benchmark for sober industry. I would arrive at Marty's flat—he and Jill lived in a succession of flats in Toronto's Annex neighbourhood, which services the university's student and faculty population—late in the morning. We would share a coffee, discuss the travails of the Maple Leafs (though back then the Leafs didn't have nearly as many travails as they do now), and then uncase our guitars. We would spend quite a few minutes tuning, since Martin had a twelve-string, which doubles each note and requires great persnicketiness. Following that, one or the other of us would proffer an idea: a chord progression, a lyric, a melody. Any one of these things could trigger the composition of a song.

AFTER A few months of this, we ventured out onto the streets, Marty and I.

Specifically, we ventured out onto Jarvis Street. There was quite a lot of musical activity on Jarvis back then. I wouldn't want to give the impression that Jarvis Street was our version of Bourbon Street or anything. Or maybe it was. What I'm getting at is that Jarvis was the stroll, the sidewalks studded (hmmm, could be the wrong word) with working women. But there were little clubs up and down the street, and one, the Iron Grate, featured a hoot night, an open mic, on Mondays.

The concept of the open mic (and by the way, I'm going to persist in that spelling despite the red squiggly protests from my computer, since it's short for "microphone," after all) is a pretty egregious thing. Club owners are capitalizing on the desperate and competitive nature of the struggling artist. They announce an open mic, and performers line up around the block. They are allotted their ten-minute spot, and an evening's worth of entertainment is assured, even though the audience is composed almost entirely of musicians awaiting their at-bat. And not only do those musicians not get paid, they are often charged a small fee for the opportunity. However, Martin and I went down there, week after week, and in doing so made some new friends.

When casting in the murky pond that is my memory, I am as likely to remember a fellow's song as the fellow himself. Everyone had a repertoire, some originals and a few covers to get the people going. (Bob Dylan's "I Shall Be Released" was often trotted out, a surefire sing-along crowd-pleaser.) But at the same time, everyone had one special song that accompanied them like a familiar. The Iron Grate was much like the cigar box banjo competition, with each individual plucking out the tune he or she had composed on the road to the fairground. Each singer-songwriter seemed to have one song that "worked." It is relatively easy, I think, to write a good lyric, to craft a nice melody. But songs only approach goodness when the melody manages to pull a syllable out of line and make it howl and keen. Songs work when the lyrical content informs the music and gives it a precise and nuanced emotional shade.

There was a fellow named Bryan Way, whose song was entitled "One John Ferguson." We met Bryan our first night at the Iron Grate. As he took to the stage, gap-toothed and large-beaked, he found it hard to contain his nervous energy. "You want something to laugh and heckle at," he informed the audience in a thick Newfoundland accent, "I'll give you something to laugh and heckle at." He banged away on his guitar and ululated, and the audience, um, laughed and heckled. But then Bryan managed to calm down, and he started playing his song, a muted evocation of a common man's life and death, the lyrics framed as a police report: *"One John Ferguson, age fifty-four / death due to heart attack / found on the bedroom floor."* Bryan also managed to employ the word "barque." I can't remember how, but I was very impressed with that. Quarrington/Worthy later incorporated that song into our repertoire, and Bryan went on to meet with some success. One of his songs was recorded by Roger Whittaker, which is a mixed blessing, I suppose. I actually like Roger Whittaker quite a bit, but back then announcing that Whittaker had covered one of your tunes was a little like announcing that you'd gotten a hummer from a school teacher, and I'm talking your own Grade 2 teacher, that sweet Miss Paisley.

Another fellow I remember well—despite the fact that I just had to phone Marty to be reminded of the guy's name, Bruce Miller—had a song called "Anna Marie." Miller was a romantic figure, I thought, dark and handsome and something of a loner. He always came late, sneaking in the door and then standing in the shadows. He wore a leather jacket, and his guitar case was battered and held together by "Fragile" stickers, as though it had spent most of its life in the travel compartment of an old freight train. Miller rarely had to stand around long before taking the stage. It was as though everyone was eager for him to play his song. The crowd would fall silent, the owners would set aside the money they were counting, the wait staff would stop ferrying foodstuffs and stand quiet. *"Oh, Anna Marie, don't you love me anymore…?"*

Marty and I didn't really have "our" song. We'd written some pretty good ones, and our friends would advocate for one or the other. Jill liked "Winter Weather Bound," our buddy Fedderson was fond of "Mary Cargill," Marie-Christine liked "Welcome." They weren't united in their enthusiasm. We had yet to write "the song." But that was okay; years stretched out in front of us.

MANY TIMES since D-Day, people have asked if I believe in miracles. They are asking, really, if I believe the stories wherein tumours simply vanish, or a change in diet or tea made from tea-bark causes a total remission. I hear an awful lot of those stories, let me tell you. Everyone seems to know one, and they are eager that I hear them. I listen and nod, and when they ask, "Do you believe in miracles?" I assure them that I do. I am being disingenuous, to a degree. In my own thinking on such matters, I am more likely to choose the word "anomalous" than the word "miraculous." Human beings have tools, medical and spiritual and even magical, to deal with illness. So anomalies certainly occur. I have every intention of being an anomaly. Indeed, I began the process as one, burly and beefy and seeming as unlike a cancer patient as one could be.

But the miracles I truly believe in are of a different order. They are closer in spirit to what used to happen whenever Donny Sinclair sang at the Brunswick House. On the days Marty and I wrote songs together, we ended quite a few of our evenings at the Brunswick House. Okay, *every* evening. We were such regulars that Belle, one of several matronly waitresses, extended us credit. She didn't let us run the tab around the block or anything, but if we were penniless, and often we were, we knew that we could still drink massive amounts of draft beer. Many of our friends drank at the Brunswick as well, so while an evening might start out with just Martin and me instructing Belle to cover our tabletop with eight-ounce draft glasses, it could easily end up with fifteen or twenty of us clustered together, university students, writers and poets, actors and clowns. We would all applaud madly for the entertainment.

Back then, the entertainment policy at the Brunswick House was to have a standing open mic, but that was something of a technicality. There were relatively few occasions when a stranger demanded stage time and was granted it. The evenings were hosted by a woman named Irene, and she would introduce the acts, even though there was no real reason to. We all knew what was going to happen. Around about nine o'clock a very slender middle-aged man would take the stage. He wore a blazer and a tie, and he had taken care to make certain that his shoes were well polished. The person behind the organ (I'm trying to remember who it was; perhaps my memory is challenged because I couldn't see him or her behind the great hulking instrument) would draw out some chords, and the well-dressed (but somehow sad-seeming) middle-aged man would begin shooting out his left hand, his fingers snapping to the beat. He would hold the microphone to his mouth as though it were a delicate scientific instrument measuring the lightness of his breath. "Chicago, Chicago, that's my kind of town..." Next, Diamond Lil, one of the waitresses, would set down her silver tray and unclasp the moneybelt that girded her. She would plump and fluff her hair before taking to the stage. Arriving there, Lil would grab the microphone and, without introduction or fanfare, sing the oddest version of "Bill Bailey" that I have ever heard. I don't know if I can describe it—although I can render it faithfully, as can Martin and any of the other Brunswick regulars—other than to tell you that Lil placed stress at very unexpected places. I guess what she was doing, musically speaking, was counting a couple of beats between her phrases. Try singing "Won't you come home, Bill Bailey?" and then silently count "one, two" before repeating, "Won't you come home?" It sounds unnatural, as you'll see. Still, we would all sing along, and some nights there might be a couple of hundred people in the place. Everybody knew where the quirks would occur, and we knew that at the end of the chorus, we would be forced, like Lil, to eliminate the word "Bill" in order to get all the lyrics in, so that the song ended with a somewhat pugnacious, "*Bailey*, won't you please come home?"

That makes a fairly important statement about the song, doesn't it? A really great song has to possess a certain malleability. Even stretched way out of shape, it has to be recognizable. Even badly distorted, the song must deliver its rumptious joy to the people singing along.

The Rowdyman would take to the stage next. He was by far our favourite; we had christened him the Rowdyman on account of his curly hair and the thick-knit fisherman's sweaters he favoured. (*The Rowdyman*, which I often call the best Canadian film ever made, was written by Gordon Pinsent, who also starred. His character was curly-haired and favoured thick-knit sweaters.) The Rowdyman was young—at least, youngish for a Brunswick House entertainer. His evident affection for liquor and cigarettes had sped up the aging process considerably, however. He radiated shiftlessness. He clearly had no steady employment, and in conversation he was usually vague about his recent activities. Sometimes he had a fair bit of money; sometimes he picked coins out of his palm parsimoniously and ordered only a single glass of draft beer. One thing he did have, the Rowdyman, was talent. He would sing "She Taught Me To Yodel," and she really had. When he came to the chorus, the Rowdyman would let fly a wonderfully melodic series of leaps into the falsetto, which never failed to make the patrons cheer with great enthusiasm. Well, all right, it's truer to say that the yodelling never failed to make patrons glance up from their drinks with a dull startle in their eyes. Perhaps it was just Martin and me who cheered with great enthusiasm.

Then Irene would announce Donny Sinclair, who would abandon his station to join her onstage. In the corridor leading to the big beverage room was a shoeshine stand, a box-like creation with a couple of wooden chairs perched on top, foot rests mounted on small pedestals. One of Donny's occupations was shoeshine man, and the other was bouncer. I never saw Donny actually bounce anybody—and the Brunswick House was certainly capable of turning as riotous as a prison during a heat wave—because his tactics included persuasion and an appeal to common sense. Even very drunken, boisterous people were reluctant to tangle with Donny. Not that he was large, far from it; Sinclair was a little person. As a younger man, he had been a "midget wrestler," fighting under the moniker "Little Beaver." (This is what we believed, at any rate, and I'm reluctant to research it. This whole section about the Brunswick House must be taken with a grain of salt, I guess. After all, inside the place, truth and lies took to the tiny dance floor wrapped up in each other's arms.) Donny had a powerful voice, and he had a couple of crowd pleasers, "Danny Boy" and "I Believe."

Some songs possess the ability, almost unerringly, to make people weep. Certainly "Danny Boy" is such a song, and it has caused many, many alcoholic beverages to become diluted with salty tears. If a song's purpose is to thrum people's fundaments, "Danny Boy" succeeds. Some of this is Pavlovian, I suppose, in that people tend to start weeping as soon as they recognize the song, which happens with the first three words of the lyrics (or several moments afterward, in establishments like the Brunswick House). Also, there's something exhilarating in hearing someone accomplish, or even vaguely attempt, the vocal vault ("For I'll be THERE...") that moistens the eyes. But at the heart of that song, of course, is the unadorned voicing of emotion. "Oh, Danny Boy, oh Danny Boy, I love you so." My own opinion is that people are dying to give voice to that particular emotion, and they don't mind addressing it to this guy "Dan," who lives over in Scotland or something and isn't even there in any tangible fashion. "Danny Boy" doesn't provoke weeping so much as *allow* it.

"I Believe" was less overtly a tear-jerker, but that wasn't Donny Sinclair's fault. It is one of those songs that seems to have been written by committee: Ervin Drake, Irvin Graham, Jimmy Shirl, and Al Stillman. I've reconstructed its creation as follows. Irvin Graham was a lyricist and a television writer (he worked on *Your Show of Shows*), and one day his then-employer, singer Jane Froman, suggested that what the general population needed was some cheering up. (This is in the early fifties, and Ms. Froman was concerned about the U.S. involvement in Korea, so soon after World War II.)

I'm supposing the others were friends of Graham's. I don't know anything about Jimmy Shirl, but Ervin Drake had been established since he was a kid (he wrote "Those Were the Days"), and Al Stillman was a newspaperman and a staff writer at Radio City Music Hall. Jane Froman first recorded "I Believe," although Frankie Laine had the biggest hit with it. Other covers included renditions by the Righteous Brothers, the Young Rascals, Mahalia Jackson, and Elvis Presley.

I think Donny Sinclair was most influenced by the King. Not that he did any pelvic thrusting, but he sang with his voice deep in his throat, with a kind of humble sincerity, which is how Elvis addressed each of the many gospel songs he recorded. Toward the end of "I Believe," Donny would motion somewhat irritably in the direction of the organist, as if silencing a full string and woodwind section. In the resulting hush, he would press the microphone to his lips and pronounce: "You know, ladies and gentleman, every so often I make the mistake of feeling sorry for myself. I think that everyone else is out having a good time, and I'm not. But you know what? They're not all having a good time. There's a lot of lonely people out there! That's why *Every time I hear a new-born baby cry...*"

At the end of the song, I would weep and applaud very loudly.

Over time, my applause convinced Donny Sinclair— "The Little Man with the Big Voice"—that I, and by association Martin, held profound religious beliefs. He had heard us singing harmony, sitting at our table and bellowing with inebriated dedication, and one night he invited us up onstage to sing the glorious spiritual "Amazing Grace." There was only one microphone, which Donny wielded, so Marty and I crouched beside him as he waved the thing in the air, trying to effect a compromise among the various mouth levels.

I don't actually hold profound religious beliefs, as you may have deduced. I wasn't applauding "I Believe" because of its religious overtones. After all, it's not especially Christian to cheer oneself up, as Donny urged in his little speech, by thinking about all the unfortunates who are worse off. (It's very human, of course; I do it all the time.) I applauded the song precisely because it was *non*-religious, at least non-biblical, non-churchgoing. This fact likely has its roots in the committee who wrote it. Not only were some members Jewish, but a committee will naturally have a problem giving precise voice to spiritual matters, because everyone has a slightly different idea of what might go on in what the song refers to as "the great somewhere."

What I liked about the song was that it makes miraculous the mundane. It may have been mathematical precision that Donny and the committee were stressing, each drop of rain accounting for a single bud. Martin and I tried out that idea in the chorus to a song we wrote called "A Mansion of the Wind":

God ain't dead, he's not to blame.
But He has to spend all his time making snowflakes not the same.

But really, I've never needed to imagine His Great Hand behind the scenes to appreciate that the growth of a flower is a remarkable thing. And if there is a God overseeing all these snowflakes and flowers, He must be way too busy to worry about us.

CHAPTER

[**7**]

MARTY AND I decided we'd make a demo tape.

That's how things worked in the olden days. One would go into a small studio and record three or four songs as a demonstration (demo=demonstration) to the big record companies of how brilliant those songs were, how they would (with the proper production and arrangement) become big, boffo number-one hits! Nowadays, the practice is little seen, being as digital technology has driven the little recording studios out of business and is currently taking aim at the big ones. Simply put, anyone now has the capability to make a professional-sounding recording. Indeed, fairly advanced software is on many people's computers without their even knowing it. This machine I'm currently pounding on, for example, comes out of the shop with Garage Band, a reasonably sophisticated program, already installed. But back then we were dealing with magnetic tape, and sounds had to be scratched upon that tape in some fashion only a few wizards understood. Quarrington/Worthy got a couple of friends to back us up (the bass was played by our old friend Stephen Tulk), and we went into a recording studio.

Mike Burke located the studio. You recall Mickle Burkle from pages previous, I trust, the bearded, sweat-shirted computer nerd who these days owns a record company and lives in a house so large and fabulous I don't think he'd notice if I moved in. (That, in a nutshell, used to be my retirement plan. But I don't need a retirement plan no more.) Burkie didn't have a lot of money back then, when we were all in our twenties, but he had a real job, a good one, and accordingly had a lot more money than the rest of us. He was searching for some attachment to the arts, and seeing as Martin and I were both old friends of his (he and Marty have known each other since the age of six), he decided to become our angel. We didn't use that terminology, of course. We may even have referred to Burkle as our "manager," although we needed little management—it's not hard to book free gigs, and Marty and I drank so much beer that we were eagerly welcomed by club owners at open mics—and would not brook the little management that was attempted. Mickle was our patron, really, owing to his having, as I say, more money than we had.

Oh, he also had a car, which is significant, as the studio he located was in Ancaster, Ontario, just the other side (from Toronto) of Hamilton. It was very affordable, this studio, because it was new and small. Two brothers had built it in the basement of their mother's home. We drove out there one day and were greeted by the elder brother, who shook our hands solemnly as he introduced himself. "Hello, I'm Bob Lanois," he said, dipping his head in a gracious manner. "Welcome to our studio." He turned and spread his hands expansively, indicating the grandeur of the enterprise.

It really was not all that grand. There was a little enclosed studio—the actual recording floor—and there was the control console, a machine for running two-track magnetic tape and a four-track mixing board. Busily sticking patch cords into the appropriate bays was another young man. "That's my brother Danny," said Bob. Brother Danny glanced up and produced a small grunt by way of acknowledging our presence before re-busying himself.

We recorded four songs that day: "Winter Weather Bound," "Mary Cargill," "Welcome," and "Poor Man's Art Gallery." But you don't really care, do you? You're wondering if I was just talking about Dan Lanois, *the* Dan Lanois, he of international fame, hobnobber with the great and fabled. Sure. Bob's brother Danny.

Yes, it's true, we did know Dan Lanois early in his career. Actually, we were somewhat influential in shaping that career. After Martin and I made our first four-song demo, we continued to record at Bob and Danny's mother's place. Whenever we had a new group of songs, we'd head out there. We recommended the place to other musicians. My brother Tony went to their studio to record some of his novelty tunes. Soon many, many artists from around southern Ontario were recording there, and the Lanois brothers needed to find a bigger space. They located the ideal place in downtown Hamilton, on Grant Avenue, and then were faced with a cash flow problem, needing to come up with a fair chunk of change quickly. Bob and Danny approached Mike Burke and offered to sell him a lot of time in the new space—X number of hours—for a greatly reduced rate, the caveat being that he had to pay for those hours up front. Well, Mike knows a deal when he sees one, and it was in this manner that the Quarrington/Worthy album, and my brother's album, *Top 10 Written All Over It*, came to be recorded at the now world-famous Grant Avenue Studio.

All of this predates Brian Eno's somewhat glassy-eyed entrance onto the scene. Eno went to Grant Avenue Studio to record some of his ambient music. From what I understand, Dan wasn't all that taken with the music to begin with, but he found himself increasingly attracted to the atmospheric effects, Eno's emphasis on sound rather than pitch and/or metre. And Eno was impressed with young Danny, so much so that he invited him to join him, as co-producer, on the U2 album *The Unforgettable Fire*. Bono was impressed with young Danny, so much so that he recommended him to Bob Dylan.

All this was a little surprising, I guess. For one thing, whenever anyone achieves world fame, it's surprising. Talent only buys you a ticket in the lottery, after all. We knew Danny was talented. Not only could he patch cords into the appropriate bays (which is nowhere near as simple as it may sound), he proved himself to be an astoundingly good musician. Dan played guitar on our album, along with pedal steel, that complicated Rube Goldberg machine that informs the most classic and traditional country and western. He was skilled in the studio, tasteful in the sounds he created, thoughtful in his arrangements. But this approach—always putting the music first, never thinking to imprint a distinctive Lanois stamp on it for its own sake—didn't exactly presage a dramatic ascension to the high vault of musical fame. Mind you, he was given to what we perceived as eccentricities. For instance, in those days, faders had to be ridden.

I'll try to explain without sounding pedantic or saying something completely bone-headed and wrong. On the mixing board, each track (as in twenty-four track, sixty-four track, etcetera) has various knobs and buttons and levers, but the volume is controlled by sliding a piece of plastic up and down along a straight line. That's a fader. During the final mixes, these faders came into play, as you'd expect. When the guitar solo came, the fader on the guitar track had to be shoved up slightly. A wonky background vocal note might have to be slipped into the background, and thus the appropriate fader would be slid closer to the bottom of the board. These days, this stuff is pre-programmed, and the computer in charge of the final mixes knows all the tasks that it must execute: at 2:03:11, track four must be dipped, like that. But when we first recorded, faders had to be manipulated manually. That was usually the job of the producer, or maybe the producer in conjunction with a trusted engineer, but Danny liked to have everyone in the booth lay a finger on some fader or another. He might assign specific tasks—at 2:03, when the singer goes "Woohoo!" track four must be dipped—but he encouraged everyone to get into the music, to feel the rises and falls and work the faders accordingly. These were probably among Lanois's first experiments in inspiriting the recording studio with some of the energy that informs live performance.

Danny only ever did one thing at the time that indicated he might be headed someplace farther away than Hamtown, Ontario. I think it occurred when we were working on Tony's novelty album. And I might preface the story with a little anecdote about overdubs. In a multi-track recording studio, as you may know, bed tracks are laid down, maybe some ghost vocals,[1] and then layers and layers are added through successive recordings. At any rate, I'm remembering a moment when, having successfully captured a basic version of some song, we all gleefully rubbed our hands and said, "Time for overdubs!"

"Okay!" said my brother Tony. "What are we going to over-do?"

There is more than a grain of truth in that gibe. In this particular case, the song lyric mentioned rain, and someone had the idea to portray rain sonically—specifically, via a gong that would sound "like a five-pound raindrop." I don't know exactly who I'm quoting there—some young buck in love with music who had too much catnip in his system. It could have been any one of us. Danny Lanois smiled, shook his head. "Not such a good idea," he said. But we quickly became adamant. "Yes, yes! Let's have the five-pound raindrop!" Danny's smile vanished. "Guys...," he said, gesturing with his hands in an imploring manner, trying to get us to see sense. But it was late, we were giddy, we wanted a five-pound raindrop. After all, no one else we knew of had a five-pound raindrop. Creative differences soon gave way to bristling hostility. Finally, Dan pointed at the relevant track on the mixing board. "Look," he said, "I can't do it. I'm leaving for a while. I'll start the tape, you hit the 'record' button. See you later." And then Dan Lanois—our paid employee, I might add—left the recording studio.

We exchanged a number of sheepish glances. "Maybe," someone suggested, "it's not such a good idea."

---

1 The lead singer sings the lyrics, but it is not necessarily the final version. It's just something for everyone else to respond to, and then, when everything else is finalized, the singer usually goes back in for the definitive version. Leastwise, that's the way we do it.

WHAT, EXACTLY, does a producer do, you may still be wondering.

I would say, to begin with, the producer helps in the selection of material. Sometimes the producer selects the material by him- or herself, and I suspect there are instances when the artist, pumped up with pharmaceuticals and egotism, decrees the songs. But usually this is an area where the producer has influence. And having selected the songs, the producer is usually the one who gives them a distinctive nature. This may be as drastic as reimagining them, taking something up-tempo and making it into a ballad, and so on.

The producer usually determines the "sound," that vague but oh-so-important quality that distinguishes one album from another. There are many factors at play here. *Where* the music is recorded is hugely significant. Studios have distinctive aural qualities and are imbued with the spirit of the local geography; a facility in Akron, Ohio, can have the same equipment as one in New Orleans, but they probably wouldn't sound at all alike. The locality can also affect the quality of the sidemen who might be engaged. There would be a huge disparity between, say, the go-to guy in Akron and the go-to guy in Nashville. (Not that I'm slagging Akron, but there would likely be a big disparity between the go-to Ohioan and the sixth-call Nashvillian.)

These decisions all have repercussions. Let us imagine that a producer is charged with producing ten songs written and sung by an artist named, oh, Jude the Obscure. Well, Jude the Obscure could be featured with only his own gnarbly guitar for accompaniment. He could be backed up by a string quartet, a small jazz combo, nineteen guys beating on koto drums, or the Berlin Philharmonic. The possibilities are endless. The producer has to make the right aesthetic call, and budgetary concerns also come into play, as he thence has to contract the musicians. (Or hire someone else to contract the musicians, especially if he wants any kind of horn or string section. This is how it happens that Porkbelly's bassman, Chasbo, has been on so many recordings by so many famous people.) The producer might also think about special guests—maybe Prince can play the guitar solo on this track, that kind of thing. The producer has to determine methodology. Is everything going to come live from the floor, or will there be a reliance on the technology of the over-do? Is the entire thing going to be recorded in a single weekend, or are there vast empty pockets of time, so much so that songs can be composed in the studio, so much so that the musicians, their heads made vapid by intoxicants, can doze on the sofas in the control room until inspiration stands them up on their spindly legs?[2]

Perhaps above all, the producer—like a theatrical or movie director—must deal with the talent. He must try to draw out the best performances, and use whatever means he has at his disposal to do that.

Let me be clear about one thing. While it is true that a producer can create a hit—save a song—or just as easily destroy it, I believe that the great songs are producer-proof. There are versions of Townes Van Zandt's song "Pancho and Lefty" that are not as successful as others. Townes made a few of 'em his ownself, but that does not diminish the quality of the song. Some productorial decisions are foolish and ill conceived. I have a recording of "Pancho and Lefty," featuring Willie

---

2   N B: this last circumstance applies mostly to the Rolling Stones.

Nelson and Merle Haggard, that begins with a jaunty instrumental section I suspect is supposed to sound like a mariachi band, but really sounds like a bunch of L.A. cats being silly. Better to listen to Emmylou Harris sing the song (it's on her album *Luxury Liner*), with her beautifully plaintive voice complemented by a tear-inducing pedal steel. But none of these variations alter the fact that it is a great, great song.

My friend Jake MacDonald is very fond of this song, and he cites it often. I remember barrelling down a dirt road somewhere in Manitoba, heading toward Jake's floating house in Minaki, Ontario. (Just in case I hung you up there, left you wondering what I meant by "floating house," let me assure you that I meant the house was waterborne. It was octagonal and had a wooden walkway constructed around its perimeter. I suppose that beneath the house proper were some buoyancy devices; at any rate, it floated.) Jake's hands gripped the steering wheel so tightly that his knuckles blanched. He was grim-faced and teetering on the brink of insobriety, a chasm into which he rarely falls. "I thought," he said lowly, "that we were like Pancho and Lefty. You know what I mean?"

I didn't, exactly. It's possible that even Jake was a little unclear. I hope he was applying at least a modicum of his concentration to the task of driving, which he had undertaken at a velocity not countenanced by the law. So it's possible he meant he and I were like "Pancho and Emiliano," as in "Villa and Zapata," the great Mexican revolutionaries. I think he meant to introduce the concept of steadfastness, of a committed dyad that could withstand all manner of destructive outside forces, because we were discussing his recent bride's more recent decision to live otherwise than with Jake. But in citing "Pancho and Lefty," he had in fact raised the spectre of betrayal. Perhaps this was intentional. As I say, he was teetering on the brink of insobriety. I should not talk; I am the one who, later that night, strolled nonchalantly off the aforementioned wooden walkway and into the nearly gelid Lake of the Woods.

I think it entirely possible that even Townes Van Zandt was a little iffy about what precisely was going on in the world of "Pancho and Lefty." He allowed himself to mix up mythologies, to conflate folklore. It's almost as though, inside Townes's fertile and febrile mind, there were all these characters running around. There was the historical Pancho Villa, whose assassination gave rise to these famous last words: "Don't let it end like this. Tell them I said something." Somewhere in there, perhaps, was Lefty Costello, the fictive union organizer from Clifford Odets's *Waiting for Lefty*, who, like Godot, never shows up—in Lefty's case, because he's been murdered. These two disparate characters bump into each other, deep within the Van Zandt cranium, and Townes imagines a tale of intrigue, of betrayal, of death. Being Townes Van Zandt, he allots no time to reflection, to ratiocination. Instead, the strange hybrid world spills out, fully formed, and the listener is battered emotionally without ever truly understanding what is going on.

Maybe that is what my friend Jake meant when he cited "Pancho and Lefty" in reference to his own marital disaster: that he had been battered emotionally without ever truly understanding what was going on.

TOWNES VAN ZANDT, who died around the turn of the last century, at fifty-two years of age, is a golden and fabled presence in the pantheon of songwriters, and my mention of him leads me to other things. Townes came from a fine family, Texan aristocracy, and proved himself a brilliant scholar and athlete as a young man. Some problems—apparently no more severe than those suffered by many teenagers—led to doctors administering insulin shock therapy. The wiring in his mind was thereafter faulty, a condition he exacerbated with drugs and liquor. As the man himself put it, "I started doing crazy things." He lived in an isolated cabin in Tennessee and emerged only rarely to play gigs. Onstage, Townes would grapple with his fretboard, bellow rather tunelessly, and quite often forget the words to his own songs. Audiences, always small, would be battered emotionally. He could be very funny—especially between songs, when he would describe the vagaries of his existence—but Townes carried with him an impenetrable darkness. Once, asked why he wrote sad songs, he quibbled: "Well, many of the songs, they aren't sad, they're hopeless." It was as though he had suffered on our behalf. I have been to these horrible places, Van Zandt seemed to say, "and I only am escaped alone to tell thee."

Orpheus—the father of songs, according to the Greek lyric poet Pindar—went to great lengths himself in his quest for subject matter. He is the only man to have visited the underworld. (Let me re-speak myself: the only man to have *returned* from there.) Orpheus, legend has it, could work wonders with his lyre, perfecting the instrument invented by the messenger Hermes. Orpheus could tame wild beasts when he played and sang. He could inveigle the stones and the trees to dance. He could alter the course of mighty rivers. And according to Ovid's *Metamorphoses,* Orpheus was "inflam'd by love." When his wife, Eurydice, stumbled over a nest of snakes, only to be bitten on the heel and die, Orpheus sat down with his lyre and produced songs of such manifest mournfulness that the nymphs and the demigods were moved to pity. "Well," they suggested, digging the tears out of their eyes, dragging gossamer sleeves across their noses, "why don't you go down there and get her back?" Orpheus descended. He played his music, the saddest of sad songs. Even the Lord of the Night was moved, and he told Orpheus, "Okay, okay, you can take her back. But"—there's always a *but*—"make sure she walks behind you, and don't look back at her until you're both topside." Once Orpheus popped up into the sunlight, however, he spun around, and Eurydice vanished forever.

It's a romantic story, and some might say I have too romantic a notion concerning descendants of Orpheus such as Townes Van Zandt. Many of these same people (i.e., women with whom I have had relationships) also accuse me of not being romantic enough. It's funny. It seems to be only in this one regard (where are you willing to go for your "material"? What sacrifices with regard to your physical and emotional well-being are you willing to make?) that romanticism is seen as a negative thing. I admit to being vulnerable here. When I was twenty, my role models were Dylan Thomas, Brendan Behan, and William Faulkner, men who swam in an ocean of poison, diving to the bottom and surfacing with a handful of pearls. And let's face it, it isn't easy to leave your role models behind.

This book is about my life in music, I realize, but hey, it's my story, and having called to mind the Welsh Bard, I believe I will end this chapter by speaking about my relationship with him. I have made, over my lifetime, a series of pilgrimages to places of significance to Dylan Thomas. I have been many times to the White Horse Tavern, the bar in Greenwich

Village where Thomas drank himself to death—or, perhaps more accurately, finished the job of drinking himself to death, a task he'd committed himself to as a young boy. "I've had eighteen straight whiskies," he announced to his tavern companions (after what observers agree was more like eight). "I think that's the record." Thomas also had, at that moment, a severe bronchial infection and an agent who was determined that Thomas remain upright and functioning through the rehearsals for the New York production of *Under Milk Wood*. This agent—John Brinnin, a frustrated poet, himself a pill-popping whisky addict—had located a doctor who made a series of misdiagnoses (he guessed "delirium tremens" as the infection in Thomas's chest worsened) and administered a series of wrong-headed injections. The famous autopsy report of "alcoholic injury to the brain" was a cover-up, because these guys were guilty of what was, basically, manslaughter. It was Brinnin himself who propagated the "eighteen straight whiskies" myth in his book *Dylan Thomas in America*.

Given the White Horse Tavern's association in the public imagination with the premature death of a great poet, it's surprising how proud the establishment seems to be. There is a shrine set up to Thomas, a glass case holding old copies of his books and such, and his portrait hangs prominently on the wall. I half-expected to see a poster announcing the monthly "Double-Whisky Drinking Contest! Try to Beat Dylan Thomas's Record!" Still, it's a fitting destination for a pilgrimage. Jack Kerouac was thrown out of the White Horse many times, and Bob Zimmerman/Dylan liked to drink there.

My Dylan Thomas pilgrimages have not been confined to the North American continent. I also—in confederation with Martin Worthy—once expedited into Wales from his wife Jill's hometown of Cambridge. (Actually, Great Shelford, which is near Cambridge.) Marty and I went to Swansea, the "ugly, lovely town" of Thomas's birth. We visited a commemorative fountain, where a small sign displayed the first few words of "The Force That Through the Green Fuse Drives the Flower." When you think about a city, any city, having those words displayed for public consumption, it makes you feel better about the world and its relationship to poetry. Marty and I also went to a small workingman's pub in Swansea, the kind of place where Dylan might have hoisted a pint as an apprentice drinker. When we opened the door, we were assailed by the sounds of boisterous laughter. Ale dribbled audibly over stubbled chins, darts whistled on their merry trajectories. As soon as we crossed the threshold, there came an unearthly silence. Faces, paled and pounded by a workingman's existence, turned toward us; the eyes, stonelike, burned with an unspoken question: "What the fuck are *you* doing here?"

This was a reaction we were to encounter again on our Dylan Thomas pilgrimage. We travelled to Laugharne (pronounced "larn"), the coastal village where Dylan and his wife Caitlin lived the last of their years together. Laugharne is the town upon which Llareggub, the fictional setting of *Under Milk Wood*, is based. As soon as we got there, we rushed to the nearest pub, which I seem to recall was named the Sailor's Arms, although I may be confusing fact with fiction here, as that's the name of the pub in *Under Milk Wood*. Whatever that pub was called, it was the closest one, so when Marty and I descended from the bus we rushed over with enthusiasm. We ignored various signs that differentiated the "Pub" from the "Lounge," and when we opened the door we were assailed by the sounds of boisterous laugher. Ale dribbled audibly over stubbled chins, darts whistled on their merry trajectories. As soon as we crossed the threshold, there came an unearthly silence. And a question came, very much spoken this time: "What the fuck are *you* doing here?"

Turns out, the kindly publican who ushered us quickly to the "Lounge" side explained, that we had walked in on a wake, the local (and physically intimidating) Danny Williams having just delivered his uncle unto the earth. It was Williams who had shouted, "What the fuck are *you* doing here?" and there was no answer we could give that would satisfactorily answer that question. Danny was dressed in a nice suit—ill-fitting though it might have been—but obviously itching for a scrap to ameliorate his grief. And as we proceeded on our tour of Laugharne, which consisted of visiting its four pubs, Danny followed us, in each case throwing open the door and demanding, "Indian! Do you want a fight?" (He called me "Indian" because he'd learned I was a Canadian and, given that I tan up pretty well in the summer, figured I was aboriginal. I guess.) Word of our pilgrimage had spread, so the bartender always shouted back, "Danny Williams, go away and leave these lads to drink in peace!" In this manner, Martin and I were adopted by the town of Laugharne, everyone (except Danny Williams) committed to ensuring our survival.

We visited Dylan Thomas's grave, which was marked by a modest cross, and tried to visit the boathouse where he had done much of his adult writing (the poems, the famous poems, were mostly written when Dylan was a teenager), but a couple out in a rowboat shouted at us to "Fuck off! Fuck off!" so we fucked off.

CHAPTER

[**8**]

I N TORONTO in the 1970s, Queen Street West
was the place to be. There were the fabled
clubs (the Horseshoe, the Cameron, the Beverley) and inside
there were bands. Some of the bands went on to great fame—
Blue Rodeo, Martha and the Muffins, the Parachute Club
with their anthemic "Rise Up"—and others didn't, but many
of them were very, very talented. There was a thriving punk
scene as well: the Viletones, the Dishes, Teenage Head. (The
latter band were from Hamilton, but like any Torontonian I
don't hesitate to claim them as our own.) Some groups, like
Blue Rodeo, were mixing things up, following the lead of
Handsome Ned (Robin Masyk) in trying to incorporate country music.

At a club called the Black Bull, a singer-songwriter named
Joe Hall had a house gig. Martin and I took to hanging about
down there, after we'd written our requisite daily song or
given up on the prospect of doing so. There were two reasons
for this hanging about: beer cost a quarter at the Black Bull,

and my brother Tony played with Joe. They were actually a trio: Joe, Tony, and George. (One could almost have conceived of the ensemble as a quartet: Joe, Tony, George, and George's moustache, which was one of those bristly affairs possibly ripped off the upper lip of a slumbering sea lion. There was a yellowing hole burned through it that George employed as a cigarette holder.)

Joe was a tall, slender fellow with a large hooked nose, bright blue eyes, and a mouth that could be twisted into any variety of grins. Regardless of how I describe Joe's features, you need to imagine them in motion, in a state of flux. When he played, his face would go through an extensive repertoire; it could be scrunched up with introspection or elongated in besotted wonderment, the eyes open with an intensity normally encountered only in Warner Brothers cartoons. Joe was very physical when he played, his shoulders moving to and fro as though from perpetual embarrassment, his hands often flying from the guitar to illustrate or punctuate a point. And he made points, that's for certain. Joe's songs, whether beautiful or soulful or barrel-housing, were usually wrapped around an idea, a conceit, something so clever it would blow right over your head if you weren't paying attention. Which is probably why Joe liked to punctuate these points; he was trying to be helpful. An example: he had a song called "Eva B," an upbeat and calypsodic (I just made that word up, but I'm kind of liking it) avowal of love. "Eva B, Eva B, please come live on the island with me." As the song proceeds, we are given more and more information about the lovesick fellow at the heart of things—"I recall the last few moments in the bunker, when I was a big man across the big water"—and it dawns that we are listening to Hitler pine for Ms. Braun. At the end, when a polka breaks out, Joe would throw one arm up in the air in stiff-armed salute and simulate a little moustache with two fingers from his other hand.

Two of Joe's more popular songs were "Nos Hablos Telefonos" and "Vampire Beavers." The second song title is, at least by Joe Hall standards, self-explanatory. "Nos Hablos Telefonos" is a little trickier. It describes, with drug-addled glee, the action and atmosphere on the set of a spaghetti western. "Someone is approaching out of the horizon / It is the fat director, he calls everyone '*paysan*.'"

The crowd loved these songs, and Martin and I soon loved them too. I especially appreciated the fact that, for all his humour, Joe could write a lovely ballad with the best of them. "Moment to Moment" springs to mind, although I'm not certain he'd written that in the Black Bull days. As we listened to Joe and George and Tony, it occurred to Marty and me that they needed a rhythm section. They should be a *real* group, with bass and drums. I can't recall at what point we decided to offer our services. It must have been after ten dollars' worth of beer (and remember, a glass of draft cost only a quarter), because while Marty could play drums, I couldn't play the bass. I was a guitar player, and my brother Tony had that position wrapped up. But the bass shares many things with the guitar; it is the bottom four strings (at least, it was when I took it up[1]) of the guitar, E–A–D–G, dropped down an octave. Because I knew guitar chords, I knew how to root

1 It's difficult to find a four-string bass these days. They have at least five strings, sometimes six, and I am baffled by them. I was never much of a bass player anyway, forever unable to slap and pluck in a soulful, funky manner.

them, which is kind of Job One for the workaday bass player. So we put the proposition to the lads, and they accepted. I acquired a bass, Marty got a set of drums, and we became Joe Hall and the Continental Drift.

As a songwriter and musician, Joe Hall shared certain characteristics with Townes Van Zandt. Tallness, for one. Leanness. Poetic sensibilities. An ability to wander through his own psychic landscapes.

Excess.

I'm not pointing fingers here. I am plenty excessive myself, thank you very much. Indeed, I am more excessive nowadays than Joe is, because I will vault ahead in my storytelling to inform you that it's been a decade since he's taken a drink. Me, I've taken a drink just now.

I often think that my sojourn with the Continental Drift was like a stint in the army, which is to say that it shaped me on some profound level, that there is an aspect to me that civvies could never truly comprehend. For five years, I travelled back and forth across Canada in a motorized orange metal box with four other young men. Loved ones back home were abandoned and ignored. Our intercourse was with each other, for the most part, though sometimes with other itinerant musicians, or, all too infrequently, with women who had a short-term rental in their hearts for musicians.

WHAT I thought I'd do next is describe a day on the road with Joe Hall and the Continental Drift. I don't propose this be an actual day that occurred in history; I propose to invent a day and its happenstances. Still, I can assure you that I will make absolutely nothing up.

I pick up the story on the Canadian prairie. We have been traversing it for weeks, seems like. There are five of us in the truck, and we are irritable and hot, because the air conditioning doesn't work. George drives, because he likes to drive and is the best driver. (Two of the men in the truck don't drive at all: Joe and Tony.) George has a cigarette rammed through his moustache; every so often he'll remove it from the bristly setae, hold it out the opened window, flick on the butt with his nicotine-stained thumbnail. Tony sits beside him, riding shotgun, although that was not terminology we employed. Tony reads a book, because that is what he does much of the time.

In the back seat are the three remaining musicians. Martin is staring out the window. Joe is listening to music. He is in charge of the music in the truck for the moment, in fact. He earlier gave George a cassette to put in the deck, and it is JJ Cale. Are you familiar with JJ Cale? He is a great songwriter, and you likely know at least two of his songs, because they were made famous by Eric Clapton: "After Midnight" and "Cocaine." Cale has a rare hypnotic power; his songs are informed by intelligence and a slow, pounding beat. What I'm getting at is, you don't necessarily want to be listening to JJ Cale as you drive along the highway approaching Plunkett, Saskatchewan. Because he will put you to sleep. So I lay aside the book I've been reading... But wait. Let me tell you a little bit about that book. It's about weather prediction. Driving back and forth across Canada is a dicey proposition. Out in the vastness, one can encounter a snowstorm during any month of the year. Icy tempests are rare, certainly, in July, but they are not unheard of. I am attempting to educate myself on matters meteorological so that I might predict such things, and thus avoid a crumpled death on the endless Trans-Canada. I earlier studied the sky to the west—it was stippled with light cloud—and announced that I expected there to be rain at about two in the afternoon.

But I put the book aside, stretch and yawn, and say, "Let's play Botticelli."

"What letter?" demands Martin.

"K."

"John F. Kennedy," says Joe.

"You can't just guess like that."

"Why not?" demands Joe. "It's a guessing game."

"You have to earn the right to guess. You have to stump me by asking me about someone whose name begins with a 'k.' So, you could have said, were you the thirty-fifth president of the United States, and if I didn't know the answer, then you could have asked me a yes/no question. You would amass information slowly, and eventually you could guess."

"Uh-huh. But if you knew Kennedy was the thirty-fifth president, you probably would be able to come up with his name."

"Are you," asks the crafty Martin, "part of a famous alphabetic hockey line?"

Marty knows a lot about hockey. His brother Chris played in the NHL, after playing goal for the legendary edition of the Flin Flon Bombers that included many future Philadelphia Flyers: Bobby Clarke, Reggie Leach, etcetera. Not only does Marty know a lot about hockey, he knows that *I* don't know that much. I'm on to him here, though. K, alphabet, K-L-M, uh-huh, Russian guy... "Kharlamov."

"*Enhhh*. Wrong. Krutov."

Whereupon ensues a half hour of lively bickering (Marty is correct, by the way) punctuated by Joe's guesses—"Don King?"—and my reminders that he is not allowed to merely guess names, despite Botticelli being a guessing game. (I should maybe point out, a joint had been hoovered a while back.) The game drags on, and they are unable to guess my famous person whose last name starts with a "K." When I finally tell them the answer—Derwood Kirby[2]—they threaten to throw me out of the truck. I save myself by pointing out that it's now ten past two and raining. There is a cloudburst, literally; it's as though a tiny cloud has split open and is spilling its contents across our windshield. George turns on the wipers, which clear the windshield with a single trip back and forth. So we bicker about whether or not my prediction has come true. Tony claims that it was not actual "rain." George points out that, seeing as it was water from the sky, it's hard to deny that it was rain. Then we bicker about the timing, because I had said two PM, and this is a few minutes past.

We need gas, so we pull into a gas station that exists for no other reason than to service trucks driven by fellows who must traverse the prairie, and this is where they are likely to be nearing empty. There is no community close by, just the service centre and a couple of lawn chairs occupied by old bogues, geezers wearing baseball caps and checked shirts. Their jeans are hoisted to just beneath their nipples. As we pull up to the service isle, they wait a minute before rising, just to make the point that they can if they wanna. Then they

---

2   I knew you'd be looking down here. Kirby was a television co-host, mostly, back in the fifties and sixties. He was on *The Garry Moore Show*, and I believe he also sat beside Allen Funt on *Candid Camera*.

help each other out of the lawn chairs and hobble over to the truck. They notice that our windows are open and that we are bathed in sweat. The older of the two—they are both about a hundred and four—asks, "Having trouble with your air conditioning?"

The younger of the two—a guy who has just acquired a new liver spot and wattle—puts his finger under the hood with the gingerliness of an ob-gyn and pops it open. Then the older of the two—they are going neck and neck down the stretch—reaches out and pulls on a piece of metal that allows the cab to be vented. All of a sudden, cool air is lavishing upon us.

"Oh!" say I. "That seems to work."

"Why, sure," says the older of the two.

"Sure," says the younger of the two. "Lucky thing you didn't drive all the way from Toronto like that."

"Yeah," the band members say in unison. Of course, that's exactly what we've just done. We've driven four days in a motorized sauna.

Okay, so we drive into Saskatoon and we locate the club—this was before the days of GPS, of which Porkbelly Futures avails itself, not that it does any good. We enter to find the same dismal scene we find everywhere. It is 3:30 in the afternoon, and the bar is empty except for the Day Man, a couple, and a singleton. The couple are arguing over some aspect of their relationship, which they discuss with equal parts tenderness and vitriol.

"We met on July first. Canada Day."

"We did not. You fucking fuck. There were no fucking fireworks."

"There weren't? I remember fireworks!"

"You couldn't even get a fucking boner. Fuck, I love you so fucking much."

The loner has drinks in front of him, but he hasn't touched them in a while. He has developed an easygoing alcoholism, so that he doesn't need to drink the drinks right away, he just needs to know they're there. He is a lean man. His hair has not thinned appreciably, and he dresses with a certain amount of style. All of which is to say, he is likely a musician; his last gig may well have been at this very club.

We approach the bar. The Day Man is short and pudgy. He wears a white shirt and black trousers. The clothes are ill-fitting and frayed, because he acquired them from the last Day Man, Mel, who had to go to prison following a misunderstanding with his ex-wife. This one's name is Mel also; at least, the name "Mel" is stitched over the breast pocket. Mel is surly, because his career plans have gone south. He would prefer to be the Night Guy, the fellow who gets to serve the fun-lovers and thrill-seekers, the (reasonably) healthy drinkers who come to imbibe after nightfall. Mel longs for their bonhomie and benevolence. He wants to facilitate hook-ups and, every so often, have one of his own, some slightly over-ripened beauty queen inviting him to accompany her to her apartment. But no, he's got the day crowd and, once a week, a troupe of goofs who have to set up their fucking equipment.

Mel explains that he doesn't know where the sound equipment is. (It's in the room marked "Private" beside the stage. Mel knows that.) He says the sound guy will be in at five for the sound check. It has to be completed by then, as that is when the dinner crowd is expected. And Mel cautions us not to make noise as we set up. "I don't want you to disturb my customers," he says, suddenly protective and solicitous toward them. "Now," Mel says, rolling up his sleeves, "did you guys want to start a tab?"

Of course we did! That is what we do, beyond playing music; we start tabs across the nation! We establish loci of trade and commerce, where liquor is exchanged for musical performance. So we start a tab, and a beer is consumed by way of tremor diminishment.

Then we gotta go pump Naugahyde. That is the term we have given to the transportation of our amplifiers and key-boards and drums, etcetera. ("Etcetera" is housed in a series of boxes George has rendered, cleverly engineered so that each box can hold the maximum amount of etcetera and thus weigh in excess of seven hundred pounds.) That we were in reasonably good shape back then is testament to the benefi-cial effects of Naugahyde pumping, because we got precious little exercise. Much of what we got up to could actually be labelled "anti-exercise."

So: we take our equipment out of the motorized orange metal box and set it up on the stage. The stage is, of course, too small, but this particular one is also higher than most, maybe three feet off the ground, and the risers are off to the side. This adds a power-lifting element to the Naugahyde pumping, and the stale air is redolent with our huffs and puffs, grunts and farts, the screeching sound of muscle fibre ripping apart. Then I attend to my bass amplifier, Joe and Tony to their guitars. George constructs his wall of keyboard, and Martin sets up the drums.

We search for power. We are like the first generation of robots in this. The first generation of robots was designed to scoot down university hallways, metal arms extended like babies searching for breasts to suckle. When their optical equipment landed on electrical outlets, they would plug in, charging up with enough juice to power their next foray.

Then we wait for the sound guy. He has to run cables and set up microphones before the sound check, which has to be completed, as I've said, preferably in silence, before five o'clock. No one is really surprised—we've met our fair share of sound guys—when he shows up a little after six. He apologizes and launches into an explanation that seems overly complicated. The sound guy throws around first names like we should know who the players in the story are. He says never mind about Mel, Mel's full of shit—

"Hey, Mel! You're full of shit!"

"*You* guys are full of shit!"

Oh well, now we've inadvertently thrown in our lot with the sound guy, but we don't care. You know why? *We've been working on our tab.*

Indeed, by this time our collective bar tab has achieved the heft of any old indenture. Soon we will be owing *them* money, soon we will be paying out of our pockets in order to take the stage. But we are all muzzy, and afternoon beer drinking often makes the outside world seem sunnier. We don't care if Mel hates us, and we don't care if we're late with sound check and must perforce alarm the diners. There's precious little food to be seen, anyway; a few more people have come to drink. Men wrap big hammy fingers around beer glasses. Women poke at their mixed drinks with plastic straws.

The sound guy is slender to the point of emaciation. He evidently needs a cigarette in his mouth in order to breathe. If unadulterated oxygen were to enter his lungs, it might over-load his system, flood him out, something like that. He works with great care and attention. If he were to wire the sound imperfectly—plug the lead vocal mic into channel 2 as opposed to 1—life as we know it would presumably come to an end. So it is approximately eight o'clock when we begin sound check.[3]

Here's how sound checks go. The sound guy takes his posi-tion behind the board, which is usually some distance from the stage, typically at the back of the room, so that the sound guy can gauge how the music is inhabiting the space. He starts playing with the knobs on the board. A roaring squall of feedback announces that he is ready to proceed. The band senselessly takes to the stage. "Senselessly" on two counts: that roaring squall of feedback was very intense, and we know full well that the majority of us will not be needed for a long while, because the first thing that happens is the sound guy says, "Okay, the kick." There is sometimes a talk-back sys-tem, so that the sound man's voice issues forth from the moni-tors, but in the kind of clubs we play, that is rare. Mostly the sound guy just says, "Okay, the kick," and we don't hear him (because he's in the back of the room), and then he gets mad and shouts, "Kick!"

Kick=bass drum. The big drum that used to be strapped on and belly-borne. Remember good old Haywire Mac back there on the street corner in Spokane? I hope you pictured him smacking at that drum with a mallet. In a modern drum kit, the mallet is worked by the drummer's foot. He flattens a pedal, and a system of levers and springs drives the mallet against the drum skin. That's why it's called "the kick."

3 But we don't care. We started a bar tab!

"Okay, the kick."

Thwock thwock.

I was, in my little transcription there, tempted to fool around with type and font size to indicate that the sound guy transforms the sound of the bass drum by adjusting his knobs. But in all my years as a musician, I have never really heard the difference between the first bass thwock and the last, which happens, on average, about ten minutes later.

"Okay, floor tom."

...

"Floor tom!"

Thwock thwock.

The rest of us stand around while this is going on, smoking cigarettes, working on our tab. Occasionally, boredom drives us to sneak up the volume on our amps, softly stroke out a riff.

"Just the floor tom, please!"

Eventually it registers on the bar's patrons that, for the past while, a loud thwock has been sounding in their brains. Perhaps at first they dismissed it as symptomatic of a hangover. Then they realized they were still drunk, so what the fawk is with this thwock? They start to get nasty, which is why Mel wanted to accomplish all this early and quietly. "What the fawk?" they holler.

"Rack toms."

· · ·

"Rack toms!"

"What the fawk?"

Thwock thwock.

Eventually—really, eventually—the drum kit has been sound-checked. Then it's time for the bass. I turn up my amp, fiddle with the knobs on the amp and the instrument itself, place my fingers on the strings and produce a low E, the great fundament of rock'n'roll.

"Okay, good. Keyboards."

Perhaps I exaggerate, but sound guys do really spend most of their time with the drums, which pisses me off as both a former bass player and a fellow whose brain has been thwocked repeatedly. Indeed, I'd often catch a glimpse of myself in the future, sitting at a small round table in the shadows of some licensed establishment, nursing a beer and a shot of whisky, minding my own business, when . . .

Thwock thwock thwock thwock thwock thwock thwock thwock thwock thwock thwock thwock thwock thwock thwock thwock thwock thwock 'thwock thwock thwock thwock thwock thwock thwock.

"What the fawk?!" I would roar.

Sound check completed, we must attempt to eat dinner in the twelve minutes remaining before our scheduled start time of nine o'clock. There is some agreement with management that gives us a break on our food, but that only adds to our collective indenture.

Finally, we take to the stage—this both confuses and angers the patrons, who thought, gratefully, that we had abandoned it moments before—and begin our set. Our opening number is something lively and up-tempo—"My Imagination and Me," sometimes, or "More Cold Drinks"—and people don't know what to make of it. When the music ends, it's obvious that the notion of applause has never entered their minds. They simply stare forward, too stunned to even blink. "Thank you very much, ladies and gentlemen," Joe calls out. Deciding that they've been suitably warmed up, he launches into "Eva B," the song with the goose-stepping Hitler impersonation.

We've got a four-set contract—four forty-minute sets, separated by twenty-minute breaks. The break between the third and the fourth set is always a lot longer than twenty minutes, and we take to the stage clutching beer and shot glasses to our chests. Between songs we demand, over the PA system, to know if we've missed last call, and when the bartender shouts it out (by now it's the gregarious and philosophical Night Guy, Frank), Joe orders from the stage on our behalf, a massive order which, over time, has evolved into this telling and eloquent phrase: "The top shelf in a pail."

Over the course of the evening, young people have ventured in, and by midnight the place is crawling with 'em, young people who hear in Joe's music the plaintive love song of the circus geek, the anthem of the addled. When we play our last song—"Nos Hablos Telefonos"—they roar with approval. They respond to the final *cha-cha-cha* by lurching to their feet, clapping their hands together with rhythmic precision, or at least with concentration, because by this point in the evening no one in the joint could clap their hands properly, certainly never to the satisfaction of any law enforcement official delivering a roadside sobriety test.

Then it's time for the after-party. This is rarely anything organized, although we can count on a bespectacled fellow sidling up to the band and asking, "Did anybody want to get stoned?"

Of course we did! That is what our group is all about: music, starting tabs, and getting stoned.

IN THOSE days, a typical club date was a week long, Monday through Saturday, leaving Sunday available for travel to the next town. The crowds would grow exponentially—through word of mouth, sometimes a mention in an entertainment column, very occasionally a review—and the weekend could be a little bit crazy. A little bit crazy, as in, you would wake up not knowing where you were, who that was, or what your foot was covered with.

This all takes its toll, spiritually. I can be more precise. After five years of this sort of thing, my spirit was about the size of a postage stamp. Just a regular little stamp for local mail. Martin and I had kept our duo going, and very often when Joe Hall and the Continental Drift had a week off, Quarrington/Worthy played a club date. Once, Joe and the boys left us in Ottawa. The band had played downstairs, in the "rock room," and now Marty and I were playing upstairs in the same establishment, where there was a softer music policy. The music policy might have been softer, but the drugs weren't, and of course Martin and I were always quite partial to the drink. Once a young woman asked us, "Are you guys Baha'i?"

The girl's boyfriend rolled his eyes. "Just 'cause they sound like Seals and Crofts doesn't means they're Baha'i."

But she was persistent. "Are you guys Baha'i?"

"No," answered Martin. "We're B'drunk."

Neither of my musical careers was doing very well. Promise called to us from a great distance, like the sirens singing to sailors. One of the songs from our Quarrington/Worthy album was actually a number one hit. That should have an asterisk—a number one hit*—just like Roger Maris's tainted record. A periodical called RPM, the official organ of Canada's music industry, had a number of charts rating songs that played on various formats. Our song, "Baby and the Blues," was—for one week and one week only—at the top of the AOR chart. AOR meant "adult-oriented," which I suspect translated as "the people listening to these radio stations, even if they absolutely *hate* a song, are too weak and infirm to get out of bed to change the station." Still, Marty and I knocked none less than Kenny Rogers from that lofty height, along with his little song "The Gambler." But Quarrington/Worthy was toppled, after a mere seven days, from the top rung by "Babe," as performed by Styx. And we didn't merely slip to number two, there to feint and parry at Dennis De Young and his cohorts; we plummeted and were never heard of again.

As for Joe Hall and the Continental Drift, we began to suspect there was something within Joe that simply didn't want commercial success. Here's the kind of thing that raised such suspicions. We were in Vancouver, playing a very nice club, the name of which escapes me, and someone had managed to convince a group of musical muck-mucks to come.

There were a couple of A&R guys from major labels, big booking agents, a journalist from a reputable magazine, and they all sat together at a big table right in front of the stage.

The show began. Joe was filled with more manic energy than usual, and that was going some. He blistered through a couple of songs, and then he leapt off the stage, bent over, and grabbed the tablecloth on the big table with his teeth. He straightened out, spreading his arms as though inviting crucifixion. Most of the muck-mucks ended up with high-priced liquor pooling in their laps, except for the A&R guys. A&R guys are almost always former musicians, so they had plucked their drinks out of mid-air.

"Well," we thought, "this is going well."

Martin and I had drinks the following day at Hotel Europa, an establishment shaped like a big wedge of cheese. It was near where we were staying, the Dominion, in Gastown. These days Hotel Europa is a heritage building, and Gastown is "historic." Even the Dominion is "historic." When we stayed there, it was just one of many cheap hotels. We used to refer to its "rooms designed with the smoker in mind," because the most prominent furnishing, beyond the bed and an ancient night table, was an ashtray. It was in these cheap hotel rooms that I began writing my novels. I performed a little trick Joe Hall had showed me, taking out the night table's top drawer, overturning it, and shoving it partially back onto the runners so that it functioned as a crude desk. I would then take my typewriter out of its case and set it down. It was a sturdy machine rendered from gun metal, and looked as if it had been taken behind enemy lines many times by its former owner, an alcoholic war correspondent. I would bang on the keys quickly, desperately; I could almost hear bullets and buzz-bombs slicing through the air above me.

So Martin and I had drinks at the Hotel Europa, and we chatted for a while and discussed the travails of the Toronto Maple Leafs. (Which, as I've said, were much fewer back then.)

"Know what?" I asked. "I've had it."

Martin nodded. "Me too."

CHAPTER

[9]

"SO THEN," as I put it later in my song "Gotta Love a Train," "my life had to happen."

I'm talking about the part of my life that happened well away from music, years spent pretty happily banging away at the writer's trade. I wrote novels, books of non-fiction. For a few years, my living was made mostly by writing screenplays—some of which were produced. If I'd been playing closer attention, it might have occurred to me that I was causing many fine actors to take up musical instruments. Bridget Fonda spent hours strumming a guitar, Jessica Tandy bowed a violin, Billy Dee Williams learned to play jazzy intervals on the piano. A young actor named Michael Mahonen became quite a fine trumpet player. What I'm getting at is, my thoughts were never all that far away from music, although I wrote no songs. I had plenty to occupy myself, I guess, what with my daughters, Carson and Flannery. I did make up a little ditty, "The Red Balloon," which I sang to lull Carson off to sleep, until such time as she forbade me, with a great and petulant adamancy, from singing that song anymore.

It falls far outside the themes of this particular book, but I don't think I'll have another chance to tell the following story, so if you'll indulge me: I was involved with a movie entitled *Camilla*, written by me (based on a story by my friend Alison Jennings) and directed by Deepa Mehta. One of the film's stars was Hume Cronyn. Actually, the film didn't exactly *star* Mr. Cronyn, he had a smaller part, so he spent most of the day in his trailer, and I used to visit. I was eager to hear stories about Tennessee Williams. (Cronyn had started a theatrical troupe in order to perform the one-acts of the then-unknown writer.) It was necessary for me to introduce myself every day. "Hello, I'm Paul, I'm the writer," I would announce, and Hume would shake my hand and allow as it was nice to meet me.

Just prior to the first day of principal photography, when all the actors had gathered in Toronto, there was a "table read." Everyone clustered around a big table with scripts in their hands, saying the words I'd written, and this particular big table was in a fancy hotel downtown. Anyway—I'll switch to the historical present now, the tense of many a fine anec- dote—I'm walking across the lobby when I spot Gordie Howe sitting on one of the sofas. Mr. Hockey, alone and unattended. I approach him to say hello, and we chat briefly. "I'm waiting for Beliveau," he tells me. "We're going to make a commer- cial together." I am tempted to join Howe in his waiting for Beliveau, but I really should get upstairs for the table read, plus, I am a Maple Leafs fan, and Jean Beliveau is the Dark Overlord of the Montreal Canadiens–style iniquity. So I offer my copy of the shooting script and ask for an autograph. In a schoolboyish hand, he writes, "Best wishes, Gordon Howe." I am tempted to ask him to have another bash at it. He is not "Gordon" Howe. But I am late, so I rush upstairs and see the table read is in progress. I wonder who might be interested in my new treasure, Gordon Howe's autograph. I look at Bridget Fonda, wonder if she might be interested. Of course, I know she wouldn't be, but I like looking at her. Likewise with Ms. Tandy, whose skin has a luminous quality, like oyster shell. I consider a couple of other actors. There is Elias Koteas, who is brilliant and therefore a wee bit scary. There is Maury Chaykin, who is a friend of mine, as he portrayed Desmond Howl in the film version of my novel *Whale Music*. But I do not think hockey is played on whatever planet Maury is from. So my eyes light on Hume Cronyn, and I think, "Hmm. He's Canadian." (Mr. Cronyn was born in London, Ontario. His father was a Member of Parliament and his mother was née Labatt, an heiress to the brewing fortune.) So I sidle in beside him, and at an appropriate pause in the proceedings (perhaps at a moment when everybody should be laughing at the witty dialogue, only nobody is), I shove the script and autograph toward him. He reads the inscription, and his eyebrows ascend his brow. "Hmm. Gordie Howe, eh?" Then the eyebrows descend quickly, with much consternation. "He's not still playing, is he?"

All right—back to where I left off a few paragraphs above. In 1996, my wife gave me a CD entitled *Ten Easy Pieces*, songs written and performed by Jimmy Webb. I received it on Christmas morning, nodded appreciatively, and thanked Dorothy.

"I remember you said you liked that guy," she said.

"Yeah, I do."

I'd had another of Webb's recordings—an LP, a flat plate in a cardboard cover, entitled *El Mirage*—years before. I'd enjoyed some of the songs, in particular "If You See Me Getting Smaller I'm Leaving" and the haunting "The Moon Is a Harsh Mistress." But I think that album, *El Mirage*, appealed to me for two main reasons. One was the hauteur of the lyrics, which maintained a poetic opacity; when Webb was straightforward, I tended to skip the needle across the grooves. Also, the record was produced by George Martin, the elegant and refined Britishman who steered the Beatles to dizzying heights. George Martin is a great genius, although I'm not convinced it's a good thing he ever existed. Bear with me here. Granted, Martin had done many fine things at EMI's little Parlophone label—the label they used to release stuff they didn't know what else to do with—such as guide Flanders and Swann ("At the Drop of a Hat") and the lads from Beyond the Fringe (Peter Cook, Dudley Moore, Jonathan Miller, and Alan Bennett) to the outer reaches of fine comedy. Indeed, were it not for this penchant for humour, Martin might never have signed the Beatles. Listening to their audition tape, he declared their original songs "simply not good enough." Then, being a tit-for-tat sort of fellow, he asked if there was anything about him *they* didn't like. "Well, there's your tie for a start," came a comment delivered in a Liverpudlian accent. After that, everyone got along much better. But I sometimes wonder what would have happened had the Beatles been allowed to develop without guidance from a tweedy oboist. What I'm getting at is: can we be sure that Martin really enhanced what was startling and original about the Beatles? Isn't there a chance he squashed some of that out of them? I'm certain he was fair and democratic in the studio. Still ...

Nonetheless, that Sir George Martin was capable of great feats of musical thaumaturgy (the piccolo trumpet solo in "Penny Lane," the Bernard Herrmann-inspired string arrangement for "Eleanor Rigby") is not in doubt, and he performs them aplenty on Jimmy Webb's *El Mirage*. My favourite moment occurs in "The Moon Is a Harsh Mistress," named for a story by science fiction writer Robert A. Heinlein. Just before the line "I fell out of her eyes," there is a huge gushing of melodic sentiment, as though Jimmy Webb can stand on the manhole cover of his emotions no longer, nope, the sewers are backing up.

Later that Christmas Day, stuffed with turkey and trimmings, I sat down in the kitchen and listened to my new CD. And I was gobsmacked.

Let me back away from that statement for just one moment to render a more sober-sided assessment of *Ten Easy Pieces*. The production was sparse and understated. For the most part, the recording features Webb playing the piano, singing in a particularly baleful way. Webb struggles with the high notes; often his purchase on the precise pitch is weak. But he sings with gusto, and his self-accompaniment is juicy, the chords creeping with clustered menace underneath his voice. The producer had seen fit to colour each track, perhaps adding a guest vocalist—Shawn Colvin, Marc Cohn, Michael McDonald—or some tiny bit of instrumentation. I checked the credits on the CD jewel box—fifteen years ago, I could still make out the occasional line of print—and saw with some surprise that the producer was Fred Mollin, one half—with Matthew McCauley—of the production team that had contributed to Dan Hill's great success.

What most appealed to me about the album was something that had been missing in Webb previously, or something that I had had no eyes to see or ears to hear: his honesty. On

Ten Easy Pieces, he presented an unflinching survey of his heart, as though it were a transparency projected at the front of a lecture hall, Webb standing there with a laser pointer, indicating all the lesions and swellings. "The Moon's a Harsh Mistress," in this version naked and unadorned, was no longer opaque, despite the high dudgeon and language. Other songs, clearly not autobiographical—"Wichita Lineman" is about, well, a telephone lineman in Kansas—were forthright and unflinching on other people's behalfs. It struck me that many of the finest songs do this; they give voice to those who lack one.

LISTENING TO *Ten Easy Pieces* got me thinking, and something else fortuitous occurred around the same time. To tell you about it, I must revisit an event described earlier in this narrative, the Butterfield Band concert at the Rock Pile I attended as a teenager. You may recall I mentioned three older boys who were also at that concert, unbeknownst to me. Martin Worthy you know quite well by now, and Chas Elliott and Stuart Laughton are about to join us.

By this juncture in the story, the four of us were entrenched in adulthood. Firmly entrenched, in fact. The last vestiges of youth had long ago been torn away by mortgages and marriages. Chas and Stuart had become professional musicians, and as such, found themselves at some point on tour in—I believe—Spain. Spain or France or some such European place with beaches, and during a period of respite from their orchestral duties, the boys were wandering along a beach discussing blues music. Now, I have never understood why they were discussing the blues under such circumstances (said circumstances would have included, would they not, bared breasts?), but they were. Chas and Stuart were bemoaning the fact that they no longer played the blues, that there was no outlet for this proclivity. Orchestral bass players like nothing better than slapping away on a electric bass—which, if nothing else, is a lot less physical labour—and Stuart, in addition to his accomplishments on the trumpet, had taught himself to play the guitar (like Mike Bloomfield) and the harmonica (like the great Bunky Butterfield himself). The two decided they would get together and "jam," a word I have put in poncey quotation marks so that I can discuss it for a little bit.

"Jamming" is what occurs when a bunch of musicians get together to play. It is not a rehearsal for an upcoming gig, and rarely is it a performance. (One could argue that most performances of jazz music are jam sessions, but, um, why not wait until I'm finished explaining before putting forth that argument?) In its truest sense, we're discussing a one-off. The personnel are random, dictated by the Fates and the Muses acting in consort. There may be something resembling a standard line-up (bass, drums, keys, guitar), but nothing would prevent five tuba players from getting together to jam. (Nothing at the moment, that is; you might want to lobby your local Member of Parliament to see if he/she can't introduce some sort of law.) Anyway, the line-up is assembled, or assembles itself, and then, usually, a song is played. Occasionally everyone just has at it. Purely improvised music does have a place in the world; it's just that everyone hopes that place is far, far away from themselves. More often than not a song is suggested, so that the participants have a place to begin, a framework upon which to hang their ideas and inventions. Jazz musicians often look to the Great American Song Book, those classics that first saw the light of day on the Broadway stage or the Hollywood screen. "How about," someone might suggest, "'Somewhere over the Rainbow'?" And the others will nod, because the changes are well known. The song typically begins with a flat four minor seventh flattened fifth—oops, maybe the changes aren't all that well known. They are, like those weird Beatles songs I could never figure out, sophisticated. (Now that I think of it, jazz ensembles often play Beatles tunes. Rarely do you hear them jamming on "Jumpin' Jack Flash," although I'm sure it has happened.) My point is, it's part of a jazz guy's job to know changes, the chords to all the classics and standards and a few hundred esoteric tunes.

Blues musicians, by contrast, are really only required to know the blues. As a musical term, "blues" refers to a specific chord structure, the template for 99 per cent of all blues tunes. You may have heard the term "twelve-bar blues," and here's what we're talking about: I (4 bars), IV (2 bars), I (2 bars), V (2 bars), I (2 bars). That's it, with some minor variations. Sometimes a blues goes up to the IV on the second bar, and this is mostly dictated by how well the players know the song being performed. "Stormy Monday" usually doesn't do it; Butterfield's similar "Driftin' and Driftin'" usually does. If you are ever listening to some blues guys jam, pay attention to the second bar of every verse. I wager you'll notice that, for the first couple of times round the block, there is some confusion there, some dissonance. The last pair of bars can also be divided up, so that the notes go from the tonic to the dominant seventh, which supplies drama and urgency.

So: Stuart Laughton and Chas Elliott were walking along a European beach, ignoring bared breasts, discussing the blues. They had decided it would be fun to jam, and they wondered who else might care to join in. "How about," one of them suggested, "Joel's brother?"

In the world of symphonic music, I am Joel's brother. I have no complaint with that. After all, in the world of Canadian letters, he is "Paul's brother." Actually, it is more like "Paul's brother Joel, that amazing bassist, and by the way, remind me what Paul has written." Anyway, I was contacted, once those fellows arrived back in Canada, and a jam was scheduled.

I went over to Chas's house (his then-house, as he and his lovely artist wife, Alex, seem to move a lot). I pulled out a borrowed electric guitar and an amplifier of the same ilk as the one I'd used to blast out "Satisfaction" all those years ago. Stuart Laughton was toting a beautiful black Gibson guitar (the same style played by one of his great heroes, B.B. King) and a Fender amplifier,[1] along with a battered suitcase full of harmonicas and peripherals. By "peripherals" I mean things like cables, tuners, picks, and capos. I assumed upon seeing the suitcase that Stuart was a well-equipped and organized man, but I was soon to learn this was not true. Despite the fact that the case was crammed full of stuff, *no particular and needed item could ever be located*. It was kind of astounding. Likewise with his harmonicas. It was almost like a magic trick: "You see here, I have twenty-nine silver harmonicas. Name a key,

---

1   Both these items have more official designations. The guitar might be an, um, ES-135, and the amplifier a (I'm guessing) Twin Reverb. One of the things that undermines my stature as a fisherman is my inability to distinguish one species from another, and this taxonomic shortcoming extends into all areas of my life. When it comes to musical equipment, I've just never been that interested. As kids, whenever Murph, Kim, and I went to a concert, those guys always wanted to go an hour early so they could press up against the stage and drool over the gear. I would, more often that not, take a book.

any key, the more common the better! Hmm? G? *There is no harmonica in the key of G!!*" Chas, for his part, produced a bass that seemed to have been sculpted by Degas, exquisitely contoured and well maintained. His amp had been attenuated, and the compression levers adjusted with microscopic precision. It's interesting how one's personality can be announced through one's musical equipment. Chas showed himself to be fastidious, an appreciator of the finer things in life. Stuart gave evidence of a more than passing acquaintance with chaos.

The first song we played was Nick Gravenites's "Born in Chicago."

After a while, we went upstairs, where there was a vast kitchen full of top-of-the-line knives and sauté pans and so forth, and Chas prepared a simple but fabulously delicious pasta. Chas Elliott is the finest amateur chef I know.

We had opened a fine bottle of Beaujolais, and we sat there and stuffed our faces and got a little snockered.

"This," we told ourselves, "is the blues."

THE THREE of us did that for many months, maybe almost a year, and then I phoned Marty and asked him to join in. It's not that I had been hesitant to approach him—quite the contrary—but the twelve-bar blues aren't very interesting to drummers. Actually, the twelve-bar blues are interesting to only a handful of people, when you get right down to it— typically emaciated guys in their forties and fifties. They lack teeth and smoke cigarettes and wear a small denim jacket regardless of the season, the same one they've had for years. Most other people find the twelve-bar blues a bit boring, especially drummers, so I held off on calling Martin until Chas and Stuart and I had done enough lead-footed plunking and were, as a musical group, ready to head off down the road. Happily, he was game to give it a try.

The first incarnation of Porkbelly Futures—for that is what we decided to call ourselves—found an occasional home at the Black Swan, a venerable institution that proclaimed itself "Toronto's Home of the Blues." The Black Swan operated on two levels. On the ground floor was what we once referred to as a "beverage room." (When I was embarking on my drinking career, there were two entrances to such places, one marked "Men" and the other "Ladies & Escorts.") Above the beverage room was a long, narrow space, in places only as wide as a couple of bowling lanes. There were two old pool tables at one end, and at the other was a small stage.

Now might be a good time to discuss the origins of the band's name, since many people ask about it. They ask about it in this tone: "Where did you get *that* name?" Well, seeing as we were a blues band, I thought we should have a bluesy-sounding name. I have always been taken by the three-part names one encounters in the genre: Blind Lemon Jefferson, Sonny Boy Williamson, Big Bill Broonzy, Sleepy John Estes. I felt Porkbelly Futures had the same rhythm, and the fact that it also referred to some financial arcanum was an ironic bonus, because our collective intelligence was very far removed from financial arcana. When I first imagined the name, it was spelled "Pork Belly Futures." When Chas produced our first posters, working wonders with his Photoshop and such, the first two words got mashed together.

With that little piece of history out of the way, we return to the Black Swan to witness a typical Porkbelly Futures performance. Sometime near the end of our second set—when the crowd (a term I use loosely) was at its densest and liveliest, having ingested enough liquor to make them talkative and eager to dance, but not enough to make them turn the corner into snarly moroseness—I would crank a knob on the Johnson and play an E major 7. The Johnson was an amplifier with a built-in, um, *thing*, that electronically changed the guitar's sound. It had hundreds of settings; you could select options like "Fuzz" and "Super-charged" and "Jimmy Page stoned on acid at the Isle of Wight, 1969." Of these hundreds of settings, I used exactly two. One made my guitar wail like a thirty-four-pound cat that wanted inside—*now*—and the other combined phasing and tremolo to make my guitar ethereal. It was this latter setting I employed near the end of our second set, setting free that E major 7 chord. It flew away in the air, and then I played a D major 7, a whole tone drop. Heads would lift slightly, ears would be cocked. It was familiar, somehow, and yet still felt strange. True enough, it is a distinctive musical meme. Rock and rollers are used to the whole tone drop—Bo Diddley did it a lot, strumming out that distinctive Bo Diddley beat, E (bumpbadumdum), D (bumbum), E. Or something like that. But the major seventh chords imbued the bluesy drop with a delicate beauty.

It was an almost funereal cadence: E major 7, D major 7. The band would join me in playing that figure, Chas adding ballsy foundation, Martin splashing away on his cymbals, Stuart contributing harmonica, lorn and lonely. Then I would lean into the microphone, press my lips against the spit-mesh, and pull out a rumble from the bottom of my register. "Hovering by my suitcase / Tryin' to find a warm place to spend the night..."

I'd say that moment represented a zenith as far as personal sexiness goes. I'm not being immodest to suggest that my rumble loosened a few loins, because, after all, it was not me so much as the song: "Rainy Night in Georgia," written by Tony Joe White, also known as the Swamp Fox. The song's lyrics are remarkable, and the story they tell has a heartbreaking eloquence. The singer wanders around a southern train yard, lonely and outcast. Every sound he hears is mournful, and the busy-ness of the nearby city only serves to remind him of his isolation. He has two sources of comfort: his guitar, which he has been lugging around with him on his sorrowful pilgrimage, and a small picture of someone he loves. He clutches this picture to his breast and claims—not that anyone is buying it by this point—that he thus feels fine.

In that version of Porkbelly Futures, we were a "cover band"—that is, we covered other people's material, and "Rainy Night in Georgia" was one of the most popular songs we played. We did a lot of other covers—all, like that one, kind of dated, obscure to anyone under a certain age. And many people in the crowd were under a certain age, so they would frequently demand that we play other songs, songs we had rarely even heard of. We did play a lot of blues, which possesses a certain timelessness. The twelve-bar blues is a little like a canoe, in that no further tinkering is required. During the End Times, when personal space pods zip through the smog-choked troposphere, people will still be playing those tonics, sub- and dominants in the same order, flattening the sevenths every chance they get. So we were never booed off the stage or anything. Indeed, we could often win the audience over by playing something, like "Rainy Night," that sounded vaguely familiar.

We were no longer rehearsing at Chas's house by this time. We were no longer rehearsing at anyone's house. It was hard to find a wife who would abide it, in those early days. So we rented some facilities on bustling Broadview Avenue. A musician named John operated the enterprise, sound-proofing the rooms that surrounded the small inner chamber he lived in. (At least, there was a mattress there.) John had shoulder-length hair and drove a Hummer, and his taste in music was evident from the way he equipped the rehearsal space, with huge Marshall amplifiers, Gibson sGs, and Flying v's.

Let's discuss instrumental taxonomy for a bit, even though it is not my specialty. The Gibson sG was, originally, a redesign of the popular Les Paul model. Mr. Paul didn't much care for it and asked that his name be removed, so they dubbed it sG, the initials standing merely for "solid guitar." The Flying v was originally manufactured in 1957. It was meant to represent the guitar of the "future," at least, the rather wrong-headed future we were all imagining in the fifties. My, were we wide of the mark. (We don't, these days, dress in white jumpsuits and suck dinner from a tube labelled "turkey, mashed potatoes, and peas.") But I guess Ted McCarty, Gibson's president at the time, was more prescient than most, because you still see people playing the Flying v guitar from time to time. What kind of people? Metalheads. The Flying v of the body—the point of the v attaches to the guitar neck, with two huge divergent points exploding after the picking hand—allows the player to reach notes at the very upper limits of the fretboard. When you run those bent high notes through a Marshall amplifier—or the famous Marshall "stack," a single head surmounting at least two speaker cabinets—you get a sound that rips your eyebrows off your face.

So this was the equipment that Porkbelly Futures used, and it affected our sound. Why would it not? Here's my analogy. Take an angler, a civilized sort who is accustomed to using a three-weight split-cane on sedate rivulets, gently dropping a dry fly on the water in hopes of luring a twelve-inch rainbow trout. Okay, now give him a stout baitcaster with forty-pound test and place him in a boat with one of those outboard engines that is, in the words of my great friend Jake MacDonald, as big as a pagan war god. It's going to change his style. So it was with Porkbelly Futures: using that equipment changed our style.

When we played at the Black Swan on New Year's Eve, 1999, Stuart's brother Robbie joined us onstage. He's a very talented musician (the Laughtons are a family of talented musicians) who plays guitar in the style of Stevie Ray Vaughan. (See, another three-part blues name!) Porkbelly Futures was loud and raunchy that night. People crowded the tiny dance floor. There was much flailing of limbs. The Laughton brothers played simultaneous solos and rubbed their guitar necks in a manner that can only be described as unseemly. There was high-octane desperation that evening in a general sense, because no one knew what was going to happen at midnight. There was a chance that every computer in the world would vanish or something, that electricity would get sucked back up to Heaven, that we would all somehow be transported back to the year 10,000 BCE, banging rocks together in a pitiful attempt to placate the Creator. When that didn't happen—when *nothing* happened—everybody felt as if they had a new lease on life.

Porkbelly Futures went forward with optimism.

IN THE early days of the year 2000, Stuart Laughton arrived at our rehearsal space with a lick. He had been listening to one of his favourite players, Amos Garrett, and he was taken with a short passage Garrett played, a parallel melody executed on the lower strings.[2] Garrett played this quickly, probably without taking much note of it, but Stuart slowed the lick down and struck it with moody deliberation. This was a blues song, he said, and when he went to the four-chord, Stuart struck a major ninth. Ooh, we were horripilated! Inserting a major ninth into the blues is a bit like setting a ballet dancer down in the middle of a football field where the Argos and the Ti-Cats are having at it. We immediately started playing along. I should point out, too, that there was a rhythmic trick in Stuart's idea. We assume—usually correctly—that the first sound we hear is coincident with the downbeat, the one of "and-a-*one,* and-a-two." This lick actually started on the "and-a," the last bit of the preceding bar. That's not important, really, except it necessitated that we practise it over and over again—*attempt* it over and over again—and during this process I began to speculate about what kind of lyric would suit this music. Well, it was a sweltering hot day, if memory serves, and the slack-boned jauntiness of the music, easygoing as maple syrup, made me think of my favourite pastime, fishing. Actually, my *second* favourite pastime. Which made me think of my first favourite pastime, which caused me to wonder if I

2 A reference to the "lower strings" can be confusing to non-musicians and musicians alike. Or maybe it's just me who's confused. When I say "lower strings," I refer to those strings that sound in the lower register, the bassier strings. They are actually the "higher" strings if you're looking at someone with a guitar strapped to his or her chest, since they are closer to the chin. Unless the player is left-handed and has rotated the guitar one hundred and eighty degrees, following the example of the great Jimi Hendrix. There. I trust I've cleared that up.

could create a lyric that, while it might seem to be discussing the Art of the Angle, would actually be discussing something other. This is what occurred:

> I got my line in the water,
> I got nothing else to do.
> I got my bait down at the bottom,
> It's down in the deep, deep blue.
> When I'm fishing, I never think about you.

> I got my worm out there working.
> It's wriggling on my hook.
> All the little fishies come around,
> They come around to take a look.
> When I'm fishing, don't need no little black book.

Aside from the "worm" reference, nothing in the lyric is really salacious and/or pointed. Neither is there anything particularly innovative here. In *The Winter's Tale*, Shakespeare defines a cuckold as someone who has had "his pond fish'd by his next neighbour." And as we know, the double entendre in the blues goes away back to that wonderful tradition called hokum.

It came as a shock—sometime later, over beers and chicken wings, of which Porkbelly Futures are perhaps inordinately fond—that Stuart and I had actually written a song. Yes, you're right, there wasn't much of a song there, two short verses, but "Deep, Deep Blue" proceeded at such a non-clip that these two verses, and a reprisal of the first, were all that were required. So we'd written a song, and that opened the sluices.

In those first days of original composition, it was Stuart who wrote most. He wrote in the great bluesy tradition of combining a musical motif with, well, whatever shit came into his mind. I don't mean to sound dismissive; that actually is a tradition, in a way, and it points to a truth I am going to have a hard time setting down properly on paper. To wit: people don't really listen to the words of a song, for the most part. They don't listen in the same way they listen to, say, a speech. When listening to a speech, a person's mental bureaucracy—I like to imagine our brains as multi-storied governmental buildings, each department frantically busy and totally ignorant of what the others are up to—assigns minions to research meanings, double-check syntax, make sure that the literal "sense" of an utterance is wrestled to the ground. There are some songs that demand this same level of attention—largely they are written by Leonard Cohen or Bob Dylan or the best of their acolytes—but very often the tiny bureaucrats decide, upon hearing the opening lick, that it's time for a coffee break. A phrase will arrive, born on a riff or a chord, and the little bureaucrats will shrug, nod, maybe even mutter, "Cool."

Once Stuart and I wrote "Deep, Deep Blue," songs started getting written at quite a pace. Marty went away and wrote "Simone" and "End of the World," both songs characterized by tuneful melodies and clever lyrics. He also wrote "Fictional World," a delightful ditty about a poor guy whose true love has been distracted by the novels and poetry of Michael Ondaatje. In those early days, that song wasn't called "Fictional World," it was called "Michael Ondaatje," but we changed that title after objections from, well, Michael Ondaatje. Martin also wrote a rocking little number called "Hemingway":

Keep your Joyce, your Doris Lessing,
Your Stephen King, and your Oates with my blessing.
Don't need no Rand, no Jacqueline Susann,
No Günter Grass, no Thomas Mann.

In this latter instance, Martin brought an incomplete song to rehearsal. This often happens, as verses come easily—once the template has been established, and the rhythm and rhyme schemes—but the bridge must contain a new idea. Marty had roughed out the chords to the bridge, had an idea of what the lyrics should do, and as we hammered through the structure, he wondered aloud what Hemingway's boat was called. This I knew. I knew because I'd seen the boat a couple of months previously, sitting on the grounds of Papa's establishment in Havana. The house is stuffed with dead animals from around the world, and in the emptied swimming pool—the pool where Ava Gardner once did hundreds of naked laps—sits the *Pilar*.

Hemingway—*The Old Man and the Sea.*
Hemingway—sailing on the *Pilar* away from me.

And in such manner did I become a co-writer of "Hemingway."[3]

---

3   That's what has to happen, both ethically and legally. I contributed to the lyrical content of the song, so my name sits beside Martin's on the credits. But, lest this inequity seems unconscionable, let me explain that there is more to a single credit than what you may read in the liner notes. When one registers the work with the royalty agency, one can make quite clear that someone else's contribution was negligible. Basically, Marty supplied percentages, and while I'm not certain what they were, they were along the lines that Martin had written 95 per cent of the song and I'd made up the difference. Now, being an official co-writer and member of SOCAN (the Society of Composers, Authors and Music Publishers of Canada), I could actually go and tinker with those percentages, but then they would contact Martin and tell him I'd done it, and he'd come over and give me a stern talking to. Or sue my ass off, if that were his wont.

Stuart continued his lick-based endeavours, songs like "You Got Me Talkin'" and "You Learn To Love by Lovin'." His songs were characterized by bluesy exuberance, and he usually dropped g's. He also composed a long song called "Louisiana," ambitious and sprawling. The persona in the piece is a wanderer, but his personal road has ended in that great southern state. He mentions his "baby" and makes a vague reference to having "really got the blues in Baton Rouge."

Around this time, Martin took away my guitar. I'm couching what happened in exaggerated and somewhat symbolic terms, so don't take this as literal truth, but try to respond to the spirit. I was playing the Gibson Flying v, dwarfed by an august stack of Marshall speakers. Martin had an idea, a notion of how we might sound, and he took that guitar out of my hands. I'd been having fun, banging away with grit and enthusiasm. It might be the case that I'd been having too much fun, banging away without much consideration of what other people—Martin and Chas, the rhythm section—were up to.

Ever since I first encountered rhythm at close quarters—when a jazz legend set it loose on me in a suburban basement—I had been on uneasy terms with it. I tended to keep it at arm's length, to process the stuff through my cerebrum rather than my belly or crotch. This problem extended to other areas of my life, such as a) dancing and b) love. I don't think I'm the only fellow who has dealt with these problems. It's a matter of surrender, abandonment, and it doesn't come naturally to some of us. Of course, unless you can commit blindly, things aren't going to go smoothly. You're going to dance like a spaz, and eventually your marriage will unravel.

And in the case of playing the rhythm guitar, the lads in the battery of bass and drums will grow annoyed with you. They will make oblique complaints about your strummage; they will accuse you of rushing the beat. This was happening back then, and it had a lot to do with Martin's idea that the electric guitar should be taken away and replaced with an acoustic. My flat-pick was likewise lifted—at least, I surrendered it, as a criminal surrenders his weapon—and I attacked the acoustic guitar with nail and plectra. One talent I had acquired as a teenager, through endless hours of practise (like my grandfather on a train, riding a coin up and down his knuckles), was "Travis picking." Briefly, the thumb keeps up a bass pattern, bouncing off two bass strings, whilst the fingers do other work. Sounds like this style of picking would get in the way more, doesn't it, but it has the virtue of, well, it is hard to Travis pick loudly.

The first acoustic guitar I played with Porkbelly Futures was a resonator. I realize you're getting more of an education in guitars than you might have cared for, but guitar innovation and technology go hand in hand with North American popular music, at least a marked and thick vein thereof. Back around when the nineteenth century became the twentieth, some collective thought was given to the notion that guitars weren't loud enough. In certain quarters, bands were forming, small dance orchestras, and the guitar player, flail as he might, would often be drowned out. So experiments were done, placing a metal cone in the belly of the beast for amplification, sometimes more than one, sometimes rendering the entire instrument out of gleaming silver steel. (All of this predates, you understand, Mr. Les Paul's experiments with pick-ups, transducers rendered out of magnets and copper wire, which transmute the vibrations of the guitar strings into electrical signals so that they might be sent through an amplifier.) A resonator guitar, because of its the high metal content, has a distinctive sound, kind of like an old tom caterwauling in a Quonset hut.

It sounds bluesy.

Our little group was beginning to acquire a sound. With our new songs, we soon had a repertoire. We got a producer, David Gray, and soon thereafter, work on our first CD was underway.

CHAPTER

[**10**]

Davy's first move as our producer
was to call for rehearsals. In many ways,
D.G. adopted a theatrical model; first the album would be
rehearsed, the songs pounded out over and over and over
again, so that everything was second nature by the time we
hit the recording studio. He booked a place called the Rat
Space—I think the name, at some point, had had something
to do with "art," but the letters had been rearranged on the
sign outside—and we went there on a daily basis. David
would stand in our midst, listening, and then he would
make his suggestions. He might suggest that a chord choice
be rethought, a bass line re-voiced. In a couple of instances,
he wanted structural changes made, putting two verses
together before going to the chorus, that sort of thing. None
of these ideas were capricious. David spent a long time rumi-
nating, often falling silent, his brain patently firing on all
cylinders.

The Rat Space was run by a fellow named Robin, a very nice fellow who was familiar with all manner and ilk of musical machinery. Off to one side was a little kitchen area, and one day at rehearsal, a woman was sitting in there. She was an attractive woman, with curly blonde hair, but she was single-mindedly drinking a huge mug of something brewed, so we left her alone and went about our business. We were rehearsing a song entitled "Healing Rain," which we'd written during the Great Burlington Blackout of nineteen-ninety... well, I forget the year—we were blacked out. (A feeble joke I use onstage.) We had been rehearsing at Stuart's when the lights went out. Unable to practise, I climbed aboard the "napping couch"—an old chesterfield that had cushions pregnant with the dust of Morpheus—whilst Martin grabbed an acoustic guitar and started working on a song. I became co-writer when I offered up some lyrics, but I have to admit that my big creative impulse was to get the song finished so that I could go back to sleep.

David listened as we played "Healing Rain," then started thinking. Sometimes he actually crosses his arms and rubs his chin when he thinks. After a bit, he went into the little kitchen area and returned with the woman, introducing her as Rebecca. We went through "Healing Rain" again, and this time Rebecca harmonized, her voice not only beautiful in itself, but finding the most beautiful places to curl up in.

This woman, as you may have guessed already, was Rebecca Campbell. Rebecca is an Ottawa native, Ottawa having a very lively music scene. She had been part of Fat Man Waving, a group that achieved some success, as well as an

---

1 Rebecca made a couple of very fine albums, *Tug* and *The Sweetest Noise*.

a cappella trio, Three Sheets to the Wind. As I mentioned, Rebecca is a much-admired solo artist and songwriter,[1] and she is well known as one of the two Rebeccas—the other is Rebecca Jenkins—who sang back-up with famous Canadian art songstress Jane Siberry.

So Rebecca sang on "Healing Rain," and we said, "Gee, that was swell," or words to that effect, and Rebecca ended up singing on, I believe, all but two of the songs on our first CD, *Way Past Midnight*. She began playing live with us, and we came to rely heavily not only on her voice but on her industry experience and savvy.

After we'd rehearsed enough to suit David, the actual recording process began. The rhythm section—Martin and Chas—went in to the studio first and recorded bed tracks, then I went in and recorded guitar and ghost vocals (I trust my earlier explanation of that term springs to mind), then Stuart went in and recorded various instruments, then Rebecca and Marty went in and did vocals with mine, and then I went back in and fixed up the vocals. We dutifully brought little zip drives with us to the studio on every visit, so that David could dump the current work onto them. All of us listened to each song countless times as it was being processed, and we all had ideas about what might be changed or added. I'd be dissatisfied, for example, with the pitch of a note I'd sung, and I'd clamour to get back into the studio to redo it. These days, of course, there are machines that can fix that, pitch correction being an extremely common practice.[2]

---

2 The somewhat bizarre (and Grammy-winning) recording "Believe" was the result of pitch correction. The machines—this is what I've heard, anyway—had to work very hard to stretch Cher's vocals back into line. They produced a kind of wowing Doppler effect, and the producers shrugged and decided to go with it.

Indeed, it's refreshing to hear someone who eschews this process—Morrissey, for example—because things are a little more human when they're slightly out of tune.

David Gray has always been very precise about tempo. He often refers to an electronic metronome by announcing something like, "I hear this at about 84." Meaning that, in his inner ear, he hears a cadence of 84 beats per minute. (That's pretty slow, by the way, in case you wonder about such things.) D.G. weighs in on structural matters, in some cases altering a song greatly from its live version. When I'm recording my vocals, David will laud, soothe, provoke, challenge, infuriate, whatever he needs to do. He is also constantly asking about my "stance," the subtext underlying the lyrics I am singing. I once complained to Marty that D.G. required me to provide a concise accounting of my emotional position before every take. "D.G. does that with me, too," commiserated Martin, "and I'm the *drummer*."

As the tunes for *Way Past Midnight* coalesced and neared done-ness, David began to think about what they lacked, how to fill the particular emptinesses. He heard some howling slide guitar, for example, on some of the songs, and conscripted his friend Colin Linden to play. Colin Linden is, among other things, part of the trio who started Blackie and the Rodeo Kings in tribute to Willie P. Bennett. (I first met Colin when he was a kid, too young to play the bars but already something of a sensation and a mainstay at Toronto's non-alcoholic coffee houses.) So Colin added slide guitar, but he did not go to David's studio in order to do so. Colin lives in Nashville these days, so what happened was, David sent down the audio files via the electronic airwaves (I have an imperfect understanding of such things, as you may have gathered), and Colin went into his home studio and laid down some tracks. He recorded each song three or four times. I happened to be present at David's studio upon the music's return from its southern sojourn. D.G. very excitedly set his machines to playback, and we listened to "Gladstone Hotel." Colin's mandate was to supply a solo for that one, but he'd given us a choice of four, and on that first listening, all the solos burst forth from the speakers with bitch-slapping exuberance. I'm still a little shaken from the experience.

The music still lacked keyboards, until one night my cell phone rang and David said, "Guess who's playing keys on the CD? Richard Bell."

I have to admit, I expressed ignorance.

"Janis Joplin?" David demanded. "The Band?"

That last invocation was very intriguing, of course, because The Band has long represented (to me and most of my friends) the apotheosis of musical synthesis, a big gumbo pot bubbling away with everything from gospel to liturgical music to rockabilly to, yeah, the Toronto Sound, redolent, as noted, of Hammond B-3s and Fender guitars.

Richard Bell joined The Band in 1991, replacing Stan Szelest, who had replaced the original keyboardist (and owner of that weepingly beautiful voice) Richard Manuel. Richard Bell played on The Band's last three CDs, often cited as a co-writer.

I'm going to give you a short biography of Richard here. You will meet him shortly, but when you do, there will be too much manic energy, too great a barrage of stale jokes and mystifying impersonations, for me to get this information in. Richard's father, Leslie Bell, was a choral arranger and leader. I remember Richard once telling me how his father would take him around, when he was a small boy, to concerts and clubs, listening to singers, auditioning them on the sly. Richard began to play piano as a very young lad and soon proved himself to be exceptionally skilled. As a teenager, he was conscripted by Ronnie Hawkins to play in the Hawks. Richard continued to play in various groups, gaining greater and greater repute amongst musicians, if not the general population, ultimately forming the Full Tilt Boogie Band, which played behind Janis Joplin. You know what happened there, but this is not yet the time to ruminate upon untimely deaths, so I'll push on and relate how Richard ended up in upstate New York, in Woodstock to be precise, hanging around and playing with people like Bob Dylan, John Sebastian (former leader of the Lovin' Spoonful), and, as mentioned, The Band. The Band, of course, are the most famous of the Ronnie Hawkins alumni. Robbie Robertson, Richard Manuel, Rick Danko, Garth Hudson, and drummer Levon Helm formed the Hawks, then left to back up Bob Dylan's reviled electric adventures, ultimately gaining worldwide fame in this new incarnation. I would make the case that The Band are therefore the best-known exemplars of the Toronto Sound (there are certainly elements there—Hudson's roaring organ, Robertson's sweet guitar), except for the fact that Levon Helm's contribution, stuff pulled out of the dirt away down south, was too profound.

BY THE time we met Richard Bell, he had ended up back in Toronto, caring for an elderly mother. He was playing with various groups—Blackie and the Rodeo Kings, Blue Rodeo. I'm happy to report he added a little combo called Porkbelly Futures to the list, and that explains why, one afternoon in

2005, he was headed with us toward New York, New York, travelling, as we tended to in those days, in a number of vehicles, leaving behind a carbon footprint worthy of a herd of brachiosauri.

Everybody was agreeable when Richard suggested we overnight in Woodstock. The town is only about eighty miles shy of the Big Apple, but none of us thought that we should press on. Woodstock has much history attached to it. Most members of my generation were either at the famous Woodstock Music and Art Fair of 1969 or thwarted in their overweaning desire to attend by such a complex orchestration of happenstance as proves the existence of an all-powerful but capricious Lord Almighty. Or so they say. Myself, I had no idea it was even going on. Since I was sixteen years old and interested pretty much only in music, my ignorance is testament to something, likely a single-minded devotion to cheap alcohol—"Come alive for a dollar five!"—that kept me well insulated. So I wasn't at Woodstock, and I don't believe I know anybody who was, and besides, Woodstock happened down the road from here, Max Yasgur's farm being more properly in Bethel. But it was not that particular history we were interested in.

We pulled into a property, gently rolling and nicely manicured. There were a couple of big, impressive buildings there, but the biggest and most impressive was a huge barn. "It burnt down a couple of years ago," Richard told us, "so Levon rebuilt it." Richard sauntered in his leisurely manner toward the large house we'd parked some distance from, looking around with the air of a country gentleman. The rest of us looked around more apprehensively; after all, we had alerted no one to our arrival. We were interlopers, and we were on the grounds of a man who has probably had to deal with a great many interlopers. Given that this man grew up in a place called Turkey Scratch, Arkansas, we thought it likely he would employ a shotgun while doing so. Richard continued his saunter, apparently without such concerns.

Mind you, Richard never had a lot of concerns. His pace was a step slower than everyone else's. "You go on ahead," Richard seemed to be saying to the world, "I'll meet you up there." This had a musical equivalency. Many times in rehearsal, we would begin a tune only to have Richard wave us off. "I think that's too fast," he'd say. "Just my opinion." He often qualified things as just his opinion, even though we were willing to put an awful lot of credence in his opinion. After all, he was the guy who'd played with Janis Joplin, The Band, Bobby Dylan himself.[3] So we'd slow things down. The musical lesson Richard was teaching us—the life lesson as well, come to think of it—was this: it's a little bit harder to be funky when you slow things down, but it's a whole lot funkier.

A lady at the main house gesticulated toward the rebuilt barn, which seemed to be made out of a wood as dark as the sharp/flat piano keys. We went in there, led by Richard, and encountered a hubbub of activity, young men installing baffles and sound-proofing, making adjustments to the recording studio in that grand outbuilding. They all told us that Levon was around, but no one seemed to be sure where, exactly, so we milled and tried to stay out of the way. Richard moved over to an old piano, rolled his knuckles across the keys. Something about the sound arrested his attention, and

3   Not to mention Paul Butterfield, the patron saint of Porkbelly Futures!

he sat down on the stool and started playing a kind of syncopated stride. That drew forth his old friend.

Levon Helm, shorter than one would expect and as lean as a piece of jerky, appeared out of the shadows. The two men embraced, and as Richard introduced each of us, Levon croaked out quietly, "Hey. Hi. Good to know you." He had had throat cancer for a couple of years, had recently endured an operation, so his famous voice was present, but faint and transparent, a kind of sonic hologram.

"Oh, hey, Lee," remembered Richard, "I got one for you." And then, as if he were presenting Levon with a precious gift— and perhaps he was—Richard told a very bad joke.

Richard seemed to feel that jokes should provoke not laughter but a weak groan, even the facial ashening that comes with disbelief: how did such a joke ever come into being? Why would anyone repeat it? Not only that, but quite often it was a joke that one had heard, from Richard, many times before. This personality trait—a warped gregariousness, a Bizarro World sense of humour—was constantly evident. In rehearsal, for example, you could call for the running down of some sad threnody, it would be counted in, and Richard would send forth a spirited version of "The Merry-Go-Round Broke Down." (You all know that song, by the way, even if you think you may not. It's the music played off the top in many Warner Brothers cartoons. Try singing the words in the title to the tune of the most familiar of cartoon themes, and you'll see whereof I speak.) Richard also had little bits of shtick that issued forth unprovoked. For example, he would, and did, shout "Hey, lady!" at regular intervals, in imitation of Jerry Lewis.

So he told Levon a joke, and Lee laughed good-naturedly, and he began to show us around the studio.

As we had driven into Woodstock, along the winding road to Saugerties, Richard had nodded toward a bend and informed us, "That's where Dylan had his accident." It was a fairly innocuous-looking bend, nothing that would ever earn a nickname like Dead Man's Curve, but it is where Bob Dylan famously had to lay down his motorcycle. It is not clear what exactly happened; Dylan has claimed at various times that he hit an oil slick, that he happened to glance into the sun and was blinded. It is likewise not entirely clear how serious the accident was. His wife, Sara, was following behind—Dylan was taking the Triumph into the shop for repairs—and she drove him to his doctor's office, an hour away. That would make a case for the accident not being very serious. However, Dylan spent a full six weeks convalescing at the residence of Dr. Thaler, which would appear to support the popular belief that the accident almost killed him. Then there are those who opine that those six weeks were spent getting Dylan off various drugs, maybe heroin, certainly methamphetamines.

What is undeniable is that the accident was life-altering. Dylan had just come off a nine-month world tour made especially wearying by the negative reception he was receiving for the electric nature of his music. His accompanying musicians were the Hawks, the four Canadians and one Arkansan who had backed up Rompin' Ronnie Hawkins in the clubs and roadhouses of southern Ontario. At the time of his accident, Dylan was due to embark on a sixty-four-date American tour that had been arranged by his manager, Albert Grossman. So I can understand how laying down one's bike might seem like the best option. "The turning point was back in Woodstock. A little after the accident," Dylan later recalled. "Sitting around one night under a full moon, I looked out into the bleak woods and I said, 'Something's gotta change.'"

D.A. Pennebaker had shot thousands of feet of footage of Bob Dylan on tour, and one of the projects Dylan now undertook was to edit the stuff, which he called "miles and miles of garbage." There's a metaphorical rightness in this, I hope you'll agree, a man sifting through the chaos of his life, trying to fashion it so it makes sense and has purpose. (Even though the resultant film, *Eat the Document*, would appear to lack both attributes.) The other thing Dylan took to doing was visiting the big house in east Saugerties where three members of The Band—Richard Manuel, Garth Hudson, and Rick Danko—lived. (Robertson lived nearby, and Levon Helm was restless, moving here and there.) Not only that—Dylan came armed with songs, old folk songs he'd remembered, songs by Hank Snow, Harlan Howard, and Blind Lemon Jefferson. The Band was game, but a little skeptical. "The whole folkie thing was still very questionable to us," Robbie Robertson said. "It wasn't the train we came in on."

I myself would argue—and will—that having altered the course of popular music back there at the Newport Festival, Dylan was doing his best to redress the issue. In demanding that The Band join him in an informal survey of the folk song, he was reminding everyone—especially himself, of course—what the nature of the song is. In the songs he composed, sometimes in collaboration with members of The Band, that nature made itself manifest. Let me support my case by example. If we posit that the ideal folk song is democratic in spirit, with a simple but compelling tunefulness that invites participation, it is significant that two of the songs arising from this period, "You Ain't Goin' Nowhere" and "I Shall Be Released," almost immediately became mainstays at singalongs. Indeed, I have probably joined in more often on the chorus of "I Shall Be Released" than on any other song. The Blue Skies Festival, that meatless celebration of our commonality described earlier, ends with the performers joining the organizer onstage to render that song en masse. Naturally, this had its effect on the musicians who constituted The Band. Their first album, *Music from Big Pink*, is an homage to the popular song, or so I believe. A song like "The Weight," although lyrically opaque, is evocative of some older and simpler world, peopled with characters with names like "Crazy Chester" and "Miss Mosey." In effect, we may say, Bob Dylan had come full circle.

I AM thinking now of a day in late April, 2007. It was a special day, because Richard Bell visited Porkbelly Futures in the studio. It wasn't the first time he'd done so in recent weeks, but it was the first time I'd been there when he did. You see, I was, at that time, very uncomfortable with the notion of death, and Richard had cancer, multiple myeloma. I had been to visit him only twice during his stay in the hospital. The doctors didn't know what was wrong at first, although it was very apparent that something was. Richard's friends and family came in great agitated clouds, some of them flying in from very far-flung residences. Indeed, the nurses in charge of that ward were mystified at the number of visitors who came looking for Leslie Bell. (It turned out Richard's actual given name was the same as his father's, which we hadn't known until we tried to locate him in the labyrinthian hospital wings.) We heard a story that one nurse had turned to another and wondered, "Who is this guy, the Pope?" Sometimes Richard's visitors would find him sedated, impossible to reach. Other times he'd struggle for the strength to cough up words, words he needed to tell more bad jokes.

From time to time now I encounter people who are uncomfortable with me, with the fact that I am tearing pages off the calendar and folding them carefully, making as neat and as orderly a pile as I can, unwilling to scatter the days. I understand these people, because I was just as uncomfortable with Richard. When he entered the studio that day, I hugged him, but it was the briefest of man-hugs, and I turned away and did something enterprising and useless, tuning a guitar that lay off to one side and was not scheduled to have any notes plucked out of it. Richard had lost an astonishing amount of weight, fifty or sixty pounds gone from a frame that could hardly afford to lose it. He was hunched and withered and weak, but he was keen to play music. He rested his hand on the keyboard, pulled out a couple of notes. "It's all new again," he announced. That was always his quest—for newness, for originality, to be in a moment that had no existence or meaning beyond what it was, a tiny bit of time where some beautiful thing happened.

Like life, it was a one-time offer.

It was wonderful, the music Richard played. Nothing he did that day was what one might have expected. Everything seemed to have been brought in from left field, and it was perfect.

He added keyboards to a song David Gray and I had written, "Sweet Daddy." The song ended, in the unmixed version, with a great long organ chord that bubbled like primordial ooze. This chord, like everyone else's final musical utterance on the track, would ultimately be drawn back via the board's faders, but for now Richard let the music sound, making sure there was enough of it. Bit by bit, notes disappeared from the chord, until there was a single note, a forlorn voice. And then the note kind of tipped its hat, kicked its heels, and Richard launched into "When the Red, Red Robin Comes Bob, Bob, Bobbing Along."

CHAPTER

[11]

I'VE OFTEN wondered why, in popular song and fiction, people dealing with The Diagnosis decide to go mountain climbing. For example, in Tim McGraw's popular song "Live Like You Were Dying," the narrator lists sky diving, bull riding, and climbing mountains as activities he is planning to undertake.

I made some decisions after D-Day, but I didn't really have to make plans. I already *had* plans, some of which involved Porkbelly Futures. The band was enjoying what might be termed modest success. We performed whenever we could, even toured a little, and in our press kit (for we had attracted some admirers among music reviewers) we described our music as "north country, born of the blues." (In other words, we were four lads and a lass, Canadian born and bred, who had been not lured away by offers from Hollywood, New York, or Nashville.) Not long after D-Day, we did a gig at the Dora Keogh, a small neighbourhood pub. The usual fare at the

Dora is traditional Irish music.[1] The musicians, perched on the tiny stage on milking stools, blend quite easily with the patrons, since people with fiddles and tambours and suchlike sit in the audience (also on milking stools) and participate. When Porkbelly Futures played there, our friends came to watch and drink and (though I love them dearly) yabber and gab throughout even the most tender songs. The crowd was full of well-wishers, and I was given much advice about how best to battle the beast.

In one of the early meetings we (by "we" I mean my medical team, Marty, Jill, Dorothy, and myself) had with Dr. Li, my chemo doctor, someone asked, "Paul sings a lot. Should he be doing that?" "Well," Dr. Li answered seriously, "there's been very little research on the relationship between singing and lung cancer." That seemed odd to me. I had a vocal coach, the redoubtable Micah Barnes, who taught me to draw in prodigious amounts of air in aid of vocalization. I was even shown a method of inflating an invisible subcutaneous lifesaver ring. I learned to blow and hum and make my lips slap together with the insistence of a forty-horsepower Johnson.

Let's take the purely practical, physical aspect. I had this sessile, squamous tumour settling on my left lung. It made perfect sense to me that bellowing for three or four hours a night would be a good way of irritating the thing. Who knew, maybe the tumour would decide to take up residence elsewhere, to disappear into the ether.

---

1   My friend Roberto Occhipinti, however, sometimes appears at the Dora Keogh with his R&B band, Soul Stew. Roberto and I have known each other since childhood, and we played together in many bands, including the Wombats and the Holy Goats. That's a pretty good name, that last one. Roberto thought it up, but I'm certain you're welcome to it if you want it.

So that was the notion behind the Porkbelly Futures Health Tour, the name we gave our forthcoming trip to the Maritimes. We took not only our musical equipment but a juicer, a blender, and a very elaborate espresso maker. That last wasn't technically part of the Health Tour paraphernalia, but Chas, our stalwart bass player, had lately developed an affection for extremely fine coffee. He'd previously possessed an affection for merely fine coffee, but an encounter with a certain cup of joe had ratcheted this up a notch; thus the gleaming chrome espresso maker. The juicer and blender were there to be wielded by Rebecca Campbell, who, following the holistic nutritionist's commandments, was going to supply me with a steady diet of mulched vegetative matter. We climbed into our van, the equipment packed with molecule-crunching density into a horse trailer, and headed toward the Atlantic Ocean.

Marty and Chas did most of the driving, assisted by a GPS unit that spoke to us in various accents, the most annoying of which was Australian; we tended to select Australian ("Stop, yer gawing the wrong why!") so that we could tell it to fuck off. Rebecca likes to travel in an old-fashioned manner, that is, with a paper map unfolded on her lap. She would study the blue highways and search for routes that the Australian would never consider. Rebecca is younger than the rest of us by more than a decade, but she is the veteran. She has been on countless tours, and she is always eager to see parts of the country she has not seen before. (There are very few parts of the country she hasn't seen before, and those take some getting to.) Stuart Laughton's favoured posture was hunched forward beside a window, a pair of binoculars at the ready. "There is," he'd announce, "a golden eagle nesting in that tree."

We travelled in such manner for a couple of days, and then we reached Fredericton, and the home of Wayne Walsh, at which point the Health Tour pretty much went off the rails.

Meeting us at Wayne's were our booking agent/manager Bob and his wife, Joanne. A few words about Bob. He has been many things in his life—labour negotiator, radio and television producer, public relations consultant—and he is a long-standing friend of Marty's and mine, as well as an unflagging booster. He is wildly enthusiastic about my novels and our songs, and when I say "wildly enthusiastic," I mean it literally. Bobby punctuates his speech with exaggerated motions, suddenly ripping a large set of knuckles through the air, usually taking out the set of chinaware left to you by your great-grandmother. During his bouts of wild enthusiasm, his voice rises ever higher in pitch, and words start jostling and bumping each other in their eagerness to get out of his mouth. Often they cancel each other out, and for very long moments you'll hear nothing but extended dipthongs, draped and flapping like sheets drying on the line. It's hard to resist such enthusiasm, so when Bobby suggested that he act as our manager, we all agreed.

Bobby did not select, as a model for managerial style, Brian Epstein, the sophisticate who guided the Beatles to stardom. Rather, he seemed to invoke the spirit of Colonel Tom Parker, the former dog catcher and pet cemetery proprietor who oversaw the careers of Tom Mix, Minnie Pearl, and, most famously, Elvis Aaron Presley. Bobby deals not only in grand visions but in minutiae. He has ideas about how we should dress, how we should conduct ourselves onstage, the order in which we should play our songs, etcetera, etcetera. We, of course, resist any and all attempts on his part to be a

Svengali. The one advantage of middle age, I think, is that it gives one the right to look potential Svengalis in the eye and say, "Piss off." After all, if one could be moulded, one would have been moulded long ago, when there might have been some point to it. So, in our affectionate way, we tell Bobby to piss off. We do allow him to deal with certain minutiae, things like where we should be and how we should get there and when. He attends to this stuff with a spectacular disregard for numerical values, seeming to feel that any number between one and ten is just about the same (so that we arrive for sound checks at six o'clock, when the sound man expected us at five o'clock) and also that any sequence of three numbers will identify the required highway. He also ignores the fact that Canada is the second biggest country in the world; he calculates the distance between most cities as "about five hours," even when they're in separate provinces, even when there's a third province in between 'em.

Bobby had lined up eight or nine gigs for us in the Maritimes, and he—as always—weighed our prospects with cautious optimism, calculating that somewhere between, oh, fifty and a hundred people might show up at each venue. What with merchandise sales—we had our two CDs and some very large t-shirts, which appeal exclusively to very large men—this would make the scheme semi-profitable. (We count as "semi-profitable" any enterprise that does not immediately render us street people.) Usually, Bobby was insufficiently cautious. We tended to draw not "crowds," but rather "clutches," disparate individuals who sat as far away as possible from one another, making the empty seats all the more apparent.

Anyway, as I was saying, the Health Tour got derailed at Wayne's house. There was something of a lobster feed, in which we exhibited the decorum of ravenous bull sharks. Huge quantities of wine were consumed, along with all manner of other liquor, although Rebecca—bless her heart—did steam me up some spinach. Porkbelly Futures, as an entity, enjoys its food. Indeed, our traditional after-concert activity has long been something I call "the Massive Caloric Intake." We enjoy these most at Boston Pizza, because the menu is the same regardless of the city. We order spicy Caesars (doubles, please!), chicken wings, riblets, nachos, and, oh yeah, while we're at it, let's have a little pizza!

This time around, as it turned out, Bobby's calculations were on the low side. People showed up at the venues on the Health Tour. Part of the reason for this, I must admit, is that I had decided to be vocal about my predicament. As I was lying in the hospital after the pleurodesis, a reporter from the *Toronto Star*, Greg Quill, communicated though various sources that he wanted to speak to me. Greg is a newspaperman I respect. As a music critic, he has helped the career (such as it is) of Porkbelly Futures. Moreover, he'd had a distinguished career in his native Australia as a singer-songwriter with the band Country Radio. So I was well disposed toward Greg; I felt I could trust him. Like anyone, my first inclination was to clam up about the whole death deal. For hundreds of years, people have been tight-lipped about terminal illness, probably for no better reason than that by speaking about the Dark Thing you may risk attracting its attention.

But what the hell, I thought. I agreed.

When the call came, I picked up my mobile phone and wandered out into the hallways wearing two Johnny gowns, one forward, the other a'rear, to conduct the interview. What I hadn't anticipated was how upset Greg would be.

My manner—offhand, matter of fact, and humorous—was designed as much to cheer Quill up as anything else. (Still, you must ever remember, the tumour hates laughter. It hates laughter, and it loves fear.)

When I was released from the hospital a couple of days later, another reporter wanted to talk to me. Again, I tried to be light-hearted. In a desire for exactness here, I should explain I am often, even usually, light-hearted. When I am discussing little pockets of emotion with intimates, this is likely very irritating. When I'm discussing my impending demise, I think it's more palatable.

Then the radio stations called—I had no idea—and again, I was, um, puckishly forthright. The informative content of what I said was that, well, I had plans. We had the Health Tour upcoming, and I assured the listeners that we would be there.

So when Porkbelly Futures rolled out to the East Coast, the venues—small venues, true—were quite full. The gig that stands out most in my mind was in a town called Mount Stewart, Prince Edward Island. For one thing, we'd had to take a ferry there, and nothing makes you feel so connected to the Maritimes as a ferry ride. The gig was at a restaurant, and early in the evening the dining room was jam-packed with diners. My stomach lurched, because this restaurant, the Trailside Inn, served the best chowder we'd ever had, and there have been too many times in my life when music competed with good food, and music lost the battle. But when we started playing, the diners cradled their silverware and folded their hands together attentively. They listened and smiled, and when we announced the audience participation portion of the evening, they participated.

"How fortunate we were," one gentleman said to me after-wards, "those of us who got to hear you."

But how fortunate I was, I reflected, to have been heard. I felt much, much better by the end of the evening than I had at the beginning. Some months earlier, I had happened upon the podcast of a talk delivered by Andrew Solomon, author of the award-winning book *The Noonday Demon*, in which he recounted a ceremony he'd taken part in in rural Africa, a cer-emony designed to alleviate his depression. This ceremony—it included, I recall from listening, live rams and dead chick-ens—did Mr. Solomon a lot of good. The entire village showed up to cheer him on, even though by the end he was naked and bedaubed with dried blood. Solomon asked a villager about some Western doctors who had once been there and had since disappeared. "Oh, they had a lot of strange ideas," recalled the local. "Do you know what they did if someone was feeling sad? They'd take them into a small room without windows and make them talk about sad things." The Western doctors made the afflicted go through all this alone. There was no notion of getting out the village, having everyone show up to witness both the ordeal and the deliverance.

WOODY POINT is on the west coast of Newfoundland, north of Corner Brook. It's located in Gros Morne National Park, but as you look around, you have absolutely no idea where you're situated on the planet. You could be on the Irish coast, you could be cruising Scandinavian fjords. Gros Morne itself is a huge red rock, the name meaning something along the lines of "the Great Loneliness." Near it lie the Tablelands, one of a handful of places where the mantle has pushed its way through the crust. The Tablelands are so riddled with minerals that they refuse to support almost all plant life. So not only are you unclear about where on the planet you're situated, you're not entirely sure you're even on the Third Stone from the Sun.

I had been invited to the Woody Point Festival, held each August, by Stephen Brunt, one of Canada's great sportswriters. (One of Canada's great writers, really, his bailiwick being sports.) Stephen had been invited to the region himself a decade earlier. He fell resolutely in love with it, and now summers there with his wife and children. Six years ago, he and Alison Gzowski started the festival.

One thing Stephen and I have in common is a love of angling. Indeed, I would say that Brunt and I are amongst the most besotted of a very besotted tribe. Our enthusiasm is unrivalled. Our enthusiasm is certainly unrivalled by our talent, which is why I was disappointed when the one morning Stephen and I could arrange for fly-fishing brought gale-force winds. We were standing in the ocean, and there was very little that could hang up my backcast. Indeed, my backcast was straightening out very nicely. But you know, after all I've been through, I would be better looking at the bright side. So this paragraph is just my way of saying thanks to Brunt.

This wasn't a Porkbelly Futures gig. I had received the invitation to Woody Point as Paul Quarrington, novelist and non-fiction writer. But I knew that it was a music and literary festival, so I took my guitar with me and announced from the stage my intention to tell a story (recite from memory, which is to say, *perform* the thing) whilst accompanying myself on the guitar. Yes, at the same time.

If you want to see "getting out the village" in action, there is no better place to start than Woody Point, Newfoundland.

For one thing, the actual village gets out. There are perhaps four hundred residents, and the festival events are standing room only. The venue is the Woody Point Heritage Theatre, which was formerly the Lord Nelson Orange Lodge. The re-appointing was done by Charlie Payne, who is as fine a button accordion player as I've ever heard.

I'm not sure I buy this entirely, but I've heard that there is a type of traditional Newfoundland song called a "come-all-ye." The name apparently stems from the fact that so many songs begin with the entreaty, "Come all ye" whatever, lovely ladies or grizzled fishermen. The call often seems specifically for musicians: "Come all ye fiddlers and accordionists and flautists and, oh yeah, we could use a guitar or two." Every night at Woody Point, after a few literary offerings, the musicians would herd themselves onstage. Someone would toss out the title of a tune; someone else might suggest another. These guys weren't bickering. Often they were seeking a good pairing. "Aunt Martha's Sheep," for instance, might go nicely with "Pat Murphy's Meadow." Thereupon would follow a musical discussion about the prospective songs. The musicians would name the fiddlers they had first heard play the songs. They would mention a little descent to the relative minor that had hitherto been unexampled. Whereas with blues or jazz, one guy might snap out a tempo to start, the Newfoundland musicians looked at each other briefly—"You all right then? Everyone got a beer?"—and then launched themselves with reinforced-steel-toed synchronicity.

Some of the musicians I encountered at Woody Point included the aforementioned Charlie Payne, Sandy Morris, Duane Andrews, and Des Walsh. Duane Andrews was interesting, as his personal style was very European, heavily influenced by Django Reinhardt. But like many a musician from the Island, he was comfortable sticking a violin under his chin and asking, "Where did you learn 'Concerning Charlie Horse'?" Des Walsh is something of a renaissance man, a writer and a musician. He was grand fun and someone I liked very much. Des tipped me off to one of the great advantages of Newfoundland culture. I am not good at remembering names. I'm not even going to bring up the lame "I'm good with faces" corollary, which to my mind only serves to illustrate how bad you are with names. I.e., here is a face you've seen before (perhaps you were even married to the face, maybe even for years), yet the memory banks offer up nothing by way of label or identification. Well, Des pointed out that his usual greeting is "Hello, my son." "Excellent!" I enthused, and I immediately introduced "Hello, my son" into my limited repertoire of hails. "Hello, my son." "Hello, my son."

"Hold on," I asked Des. "What if it's a woman I want to be saying hello to?"

"Hello, my love."

"Excellent."

WOODY POINT is built on a little crest overlooking Bonne Bay, so the walk from my lovely B&B necessitated a certain amount of upward mobility, usually carting a guitar case. *This* necessitated a lot of huff, puff, and rest. Likewise at the B&B itself. The staircase from the ground floor to the guest rooms seemed to be a riser or two too long, and when I summited I immediately went into the bathroom to sit down and catch my breath. Being me, I usually had other business to conduct. Still, this was worrying, because I knew the really hard work lay ahead.

Let me catch you up in this way. Here's what my doctors demanded, over and over again: "You're going *where?*"

"Well, we board the ship in Kuujjuaq. But then we're heading for some places that are pretty remote."

What my doctors and I were discussing was another of my plans, something billed as the Walrus Arts Float, a voyage down the east coast of Labrador and the west coast of Newfoundland (with a stop scheduled at my new favourite place, Woody Point). Passengers with an artistic bent would be encouraged by various invited guests to write, paint, and make music on the cruise. The ship was flying the colours, at least figuratively, of *Walrus* magazine and its publisher, Shelley Ambrose.

Various medical objections were raised. For example, my condition made me susceptible to hypercoagulation, which meant that, for example, on the plane to Nunavut I could develop a blood clot and then subsequently throw an embolism and then subsequently die. But I was adamant about my desire to go on the trip.[2]

Much fun was had aboard the *Clipper Adventurer*. I was there mainly as a musician,[3] and most nights I would play in the forward lounge, part of a group consisting of myself, singer-songwriter/rocker Tom Barlow, fiddler/button accordionist Daniel Payne, and David, a man who emerged from the crowd of passengers, sat down behind the piano, and

2 One reason for this, certainly, was what I had to do to get the gig. The previous January, hand in hand with my friend Shelagh Rogers of the CBC, I had chased a haggis tossed with Gaelic panache into the frigid waters of Lake Ontario by Matthew Swan, the president of Adventure Canada. The occasion was Adventure Canada's annual charity fundraiser, the Robbie Burns Polar Dip.
3 The literary arts were represented more than ably by publisher Doug Gibson and writer Alistair MacLeod, perhaps our country's finest.

began playing with practised dexterity, singing along in a piercing falsetto. We were augmented frequently by Dave Marshak, also a member of the onboard artists' collective Drawn Onward. As a group of musicians, we were distinguished—this is just me talking, but still—by the diversity of our backgrounds and training. David was a choirmaster, so he was used to pulling at the roots of things and adding the appropriate musical tendrils. Barlow not only wrote great songs, but he knew thousands, and once we'd discovered our mutual favourites—"Blinded by the Light" was one, with the line "wracked up like a deuce" or whatever the hell it is—so we quickly had the basis of an evening's entertainment. I favoured sweet soul music, encouraging the crowd to respond to me—"If you don't know me by now...".—then trying to throw them off with my hectoring Teddy Pendergrass vocalizations. And there was Daniel Obediah Payne, hailing from Cow Head, Newfoundland. Tall, flaming-haired, and genetically fearsome (you could imagine him, or some ancestor, hacking off heads with practised ease), Daniel played the button accordion and the fiddle, as I said, but often the most beautiful sounds he produced occurred when he laid those instruments aside and sang a cappella. Over the course of the ten-day cruise, I tried to learn from Daniel as many traditional songs as I could. I had limited success.

At one point Daniel called for "Queen Anne's Lace."

"Do I know that one?" I asked.

"Well," he answered, "you played it a few nights back."

Even if the physical benefits of singing with lung cancer are negligible, the emotional—spiritual—benefits I calculate to be enormous. Our little combo, the Clippertones, led the passengers in some pretty rousing singalongs, and although it tended to be a little discordant, it was communion. Indeed, within a day or two, the people aboard the ship were as unified, as community-minded, as any congregation anywhere. Glad tidings and laughter abounded.

There is an educational component to every Adventure Canada expedition, which this was, and we would put ashore and have things explained to us by experts in various sciences and disciplines. The Torngat Mountains, at the tip of Labrador's eastern coast, are almost four billion years old, we learned. They rise out of the water with enchanted austerity. Sitting well above the tree line, the Torngats are stark naked and making no apology about it. "Torngat" is an Inuktitut word meaning "place of spirits." The mountaintops are usually shrouded in cloud, and it's easy enough to imagine the spirits assembling there, going through the itinerary for another year. ("All righty! We have some squamous sessile tumours to give out!") I had no desire to climb the Torngat Mountains; just looking at them took what little breath I had away from me. Again the thought occurred that I was on another planet, and that's when I realized, no, I'm on *this* one. It has been my home for fifty-six years, but I have spent much of it confined in the settlements. I was very glad, in the broadest, most spiritual sense, to be exploring. If life is beautiful— not a decision I laboured over, by the way, more a certainty that seemed unassailable—why shouldn't one year be as full of beauty and grace as forty?

THE MONTHS that followed the arts float were lively and, I'll admit, a wee bit strenuous. I worked on a solo CD, I worked on a new Porkbelly Futures album. I pecked away at the keyboard, redrafting this book and writing a television series with my friend John L'Ecuyer. I even managed to write a screenplay, *Vulnerable*, which is set in the world of competitive bridge. (Do I know anything about competitive bridge? Of course not! What's more, the screenplay concerns young people, and it seems to me these days that I know less about youth than I do about competitive bridge. However, there's a remote possibility that I learned a thing or two about both subjects in the process.)

In the late fall, Porkbelly Futures booked flights to Alberta. The plan was, we'd spend three days in and around Calgary, entertaining the crowds, or at least the enthusiastic clutches. Then we were going to Banff for a little rest and relaxation. I wanted to eat a couple of cows and spend some time at the hot springs. "Taking the waters" has a long and venerable history, even if there's no evidence that it has done anybody any tangible good.

Our mini-tour started off well enough, although I really should back up a day. On the morning before our departure from Toronto, I went to the hospital for a top-up of the chemicals designed to push the "pause" button on the tumour. This was part of my first round of chemotherapy. The week previous I had gone for the "long day," and this was supposed to be the "short day." Six hours into it, I wondered why it was called that.

"Yeah," one of the nurses mused, "we really shouldn't call it the short day. It's not much shorter than the long day."

I agreed they really *shouldn't* call it the short day, especially as I was going to be late for an appointment that earlier had seemed eminently make-able. As noted, in the summer months I spend as much time as I can on my houseboat, living amongst a wonderful group of people, the residents of

"C" Basin at the Toronto Island Marina. On this day in early November, my boat was scheduled to come out of the water. I'd asked my friend Charles to help me pilot the thing; I'd arranged for the boat to be sheathed in white plastic wrap. The operation was scheduled for 3:00 PM, and I didn't see how I was going to make it down to the waterfront and across to the island in time, especially since I was hooked up intravenously. "The doctor is worried about your hydration," a nurse advised, and I hit upon a cunning bargain. "Put as much of that stuff in as you can in the next twenty minutes," I said. "Then I gotta go."

I was there to witness the boat being hauled out of the water. My emotions were conflicted, because according to Dr. Li and her statistics, I won't be around for the relaunch. But there was something sufficiently ritualistic about the affair—the final cruise through the falling leaves, the lukewarm champagne in Styrofoam cups—that filled me with optimism. "Damned right I'm going to be on that boat again," I announced, and it was in that state—full of hope but on the road to dehydration—that I flew out to Alberta.

Our first gig, on the Friday night, was at a place called the Bearberry Community Hall, northwest of Calgary in the foothills of the Rocky Mountains. It went pretty well, even though I complained of "severe heartburn"—a phrase very stupid people employ when their hearts have gone wonky. For the next two days I experienced a shortness of breath. I was already experiencing a shortness of breath, of course, but this was kind of like, walk two steps across the hotel lobby and then sit down for half an hour. The upshot was that on Monday, sometime around eight o'clock in the morning, two very tall and unreasonably attractive female paramedics put me into an ambulance and carried me off to the Peter Lougheed Centre. The paramedics were sufficiently tall and attractive that afterwards it all seemed rather dreamlike, the kind of thing I might well have imagined. Their existence was confirmed by Marty, however, who stayed with me throughout my fun time in Calgary. Here's how much fun I had: a seizure, kidney failure, and a heart attack.

All right, here's something I want to discuss. When they first wheeled me into the joint, someone demanded, "What measures should we take to revive you?" I was "red-coded," which means, well, that the boat could sink any minute. My immediate response was, "Do whatever it takes."

"Hmmm," nodded the doctors, and I think I had the following conversation, or variations of it, with seven or eight of them. "You know," they would say, "sometimes death can be a very peaceful experience. And given your condition, if you were resuscitated, you might face some pretty intense pain."

"Yeah, I guess. But you were thinking of doing *something*, weren't you?"

"Your ribs could get broken, for example. The defibrillators can bring about intense pain."

"Uh-huh. Well, maybe..."

"It's something to think about."

"I *have* been thinking about it."

I really had been thinking about it, and I continue to do so. One thought I had was, if I were an old car that had been brought into the shop, I wouldn't want the mechanics to scrap me just because the ignition system was faulty. After all, it's the exhaust that's gone, rusted out and rattling. I've got lots of time to be dead, so I don't know why I shouldn't make every trade-off and bargain I can.

It took Marty about a week to spring me from the hospital in Calgary. I was technically transferred back to Toronto East General Hospital, but there was no bed for me there, so I went on the lam, hiding out at the house on First Avenue. We had been forced, as part of my release conditions, to arrange for the use of supplementary oxygen not only for the return flight but for the immediate and foreseeable future (or the rest of my life, whichever comes first). Hence, the house on First came to contain a free-standing unit that draws O_2 out of the air and sends it racing along great lengths of plastic tubing, where it connects via a nasal cannula, a flexible device with nostril-piercing prongs—you know, one of those things that looks like it might be really uncomfortable and a drag to wear all the time. (It is.) I also have a number of compressed-air canisters, and from time to time I emerge from the house carting one or two in my wake. (Or getting people to help me do so. This is a lesson that was hard for me to learn, although the advice began as soon as I was diagnosed: *"Get people to help you."*) Porkbelly Futures continues to do gigs; I crank up my portable O_2 and bellow. (I still insist that this frightens, or at least alarms, the tumour.) I long ago abandoned standing behind the mic, opting first for a high stool, then a low chair. Now I sit for the most part in the wheelchair that somebody, certainly not my sister-in-law Alison, stole from a parking lot.

IT MAY seem a little off topic at first, but I've been meaning to devote a few words to Hoagland Howard Carmichael in this narrative, as he is responsible in large part, I think, for the image we have of the songwriter. (I could be wrong, but you're well into the book now, and you probably haven't come this far without dumping salt on many things I say, correct?)

The coolest thing about Hoagy Carmichael is that he looked like James Bond. That was according to Ian Fleming himself, who mentioned it in a couple of novels. But Carmichael is more widely regarded as the composer—usually with the redoubtable Johnny Mercer as lyricist, almost always with someone else supplying the words—of some of the great standards. He wrote songs like "Stardust," "Heart and Soul," "Georgia on My Mind," and "Lazybones." Carmichael emanated a wistful nostalgia. He seemed easygoing and could sing his own songs with a croaking approximation of tunefulness that one listener described as "delightfully awful." Hoagy moved to Hollywood at some point—he hailed from Indiana— where he appeared in many movies. Here's how he described his screen persona: "the hound-dog-faced old musical philosopher noodling on the honky-tonk piano, saying to a tart with a heart of gold, 'He'll be back, honey.'"

So Hoagy Carmichael established the image of the songwriter many of us have tacked onto the bulletin board that is our mind. But I'll caution you—Carmichael's breezy affability might have been a little ersatz. He was right-wing and cranky, and perhaps the most significant event of his life was the loss of his sister, who died in early childhood because of the family's poverty.

Hoagy vowed he would never again be broke, and indeed, he wasn't. The 1960s rendered him obsolete as a performer, but his catalogue still earned him hundreds of thousands of dollars a year. Nonetheless, shortly before his death, Carmichael was quoted as saying, "I'm a bit disappointed in myself.

I know I could have accomplished a hell of a lot more. I've been floating around in the breeze."

And now here I am, floating around in the breeze myself. I am currently tethered by oxygen tanks, but the connection is fairly tenuous. Often it doesn't feel like it would take much to release me into the vapours.

It's New Year's Eve, 2009, and tonight Martin and Jill and Dorothy and I will do some rounds. We've hired a town car, both to avoid drunk-driving charges and to cart around my equipment, my acoustic guitar and the canisters of compressed oxygen.

My friend Shaughnessy and I once hired a car to ferry us about. Ride Programs are set up thus, in case you don't know: the police swoop down on your car, and sometimes they will order a Breathalyzer test. If your field-tested sobriety is found wanting, they will take your car away. So Shaughnessy and I were in a hired car. When the police stopped the driver to interrogate him about his drinking habits, he denied ever having heard of the stuff. The officer aimed his flashlight into the back. "How about you two?"

"Oh," I began, and my friend completed my thought, "we're pissed as newts."

"Good!"

This evening the four of us are headed crosstown, to where Rebecca Campbell and her boyfriend, Robin, live. For the past few years, they have held a New Year's Eve party featuring the music of the Angel Band. Robin, a musician and sound guy, plays the music of those we have lost during the calendar year. This year's Angel Band will include Les Paul, John Martyn, Ellie Greenwich, Mary Travers (of Peter, Paul and . . .), and Michael Jackson.

I'm sure you have an inkling by this point in the story that I haven't always followed the healthiest of lifestyles. I need to talk about this because, well, you know... I'm dying. And maybe it's my fault; there are no homicidal maniacs who have been lacing my food with arsenic. I've been doing a pretty good job of poisoning myself. I should mention in my defence that I have made some effort toward health over the years. I've completed three marathons, I believe, and a triathlon. I've avoided cigarettes for years at a time. I often substituted smelly little cigars, though, and I guess I miscalculated there.

But what I want to get beyond is the idea that anybody's death is their fault. It could be as random as the cards dropping in a game of Omaha. You might be holding the nut cards to a low hand, but when the last community card turns up and it's a ten (meaning there ain't no low hand), all you got is squat. I was surprised when the Fates pointed their bony fingers in my direction, but I've gotten over that, since the Fates are constantly surprising us in this way. In December, I invited a friend, Cheyenne Lee, to our annual Christmas party. Her marriage had broken up, and she had a seven-year-old kid. I knew her from the pub trivia league and found her very funny and intelligent. I thought Cheyenne would enjoy the unbridled bellowing of Christmas songs. And indeed she enjoyed it very much. She sent an e-mail to that effect the following day. A little later she e-mailed to invite me to a New Year's Eve party. But the next morning her son wandered into her bedroom and found her dead.

Or my erstwhile sister-in-law, Lorna MacPhee. In late November, Lorna's nephew found her collapsed in the hallway of the house several of us had shared many years back—me, my brother Joel, Bobby Wilson. Lorna's immediate family are the very musical Doanes, and while Lorna never regained consciousness, Melanie and Creighton and others played music in the hospital room. (Getting out the village!)

And Kim Kotzma, of course, taken away when I needed him most. It's a wonderful feeling to know there is somewhere on the planet a human being who loves you without reserve or second thought; it is devastating when that particular existence is eradicated. So while I sat contemplating my own demise, three people connected to me met their own. This is not to mention those people in the public eye. The aforementioned Michael Jackson, for instance, and as soon as I saw some of *that* funeral on television, I started telling my friends and loved ones they had their work cut out for them. Farrah Fawcett and Patrick Swayze, both of whom danced with cancer. (As I've said, "battling" and "grappling" don't necessarily seem right. Sometimes the disease wants to enfold you, to subsume you; my advice is, hold its hands tight and keep its feet moving.) There are many people who danced with every bit as much mettle as Fawcett and Swayze, the knowledge of their spunk and spirit held by but a handful of others. Let me mention too all those who couldn't overcome their fear and anger, because, *oh my*, it's hard. There is no easy way of doing this, short of taking out the sidearm and blasting grey matter all over the bathroom wall. Which, of course, is the hardest way, and maybe the bravest.

And here's to the hundreds of thousands of people who died just now. Right in this moment, now a moment past, when I lifted my hands from the keyboard and raised a glass of Lagavulin.

T HERE ARE very few situations that are unremittingly negative, and even being afflicted with a terminal disease has the occasional positive aspect. For one, it affords the afflicted the opportunity to reconnect with various people from the past. Early on in the process, I reconnected with Dan Hill. Actually, Dan and I did a few things together before my diagnosis, back in those pleasant days when I felt really cruddy but had no idea why. We played together in Kingston, Ontario, for example, sharing the drive. On one of these occasions, Dan informed me that Matt McCauley was coming through town and wanted to see me.

The last you may recall, Dan and I had a duo called Quarrington Hill.[1] I can't remember us ever discussing our career

---

1 There is also a *place* called Quarrington Hill, in County Durham, England, which I found out about later in life. My brother Tony went there, being of a sentimental and genealogical bent. He went into the local and rather ostentatiously used his credit card, with the name "Quarrington" embossed upon it. The publican raised neither bushy eyebrow.

aspirations. But Dan was, I guess, more ambitious than I, certainly more willing to get out into the world and give the people what they want when they want it. I tended to be happiest in my little room, writing songs and stories and waiting for everyone to discover how clever I was. So we kind of drifted apart. Then, when I wasn't paying attention, he became a major international recording star.

These days, Dan Hill makes his living as a songwriter. His performing days are mostly behind him (although not completely, as we'll see), but he is still in demand as a collaborator. He works at this trade largely in Nashville, where Music Row is the modern-day equivalent of Tin Pan Alley or the Brill Building. There was a mass migration of songwriters, mostly from Los Angeles, to Nashville in the 1980s, and the very successful ones maintain a residence in both locations.

Over the years, Dan-Dan has worked with some heavy hitters. He wrote a song with Michael ("Touch Me in the Morning") Masser called "In Your Eyes," which was a hit for George Benson. His most frequent collaborator in Nashville is a fellow named Keith Stegall, who has produced and written for Alan Jackson and Randy Travis. Stegall's biggest hit was "I Hate Everything," recorded by George Strait. That song is from a sub-genre I quite like, basically, "I met a guy in a bar..." In this case, the singer meets a profoundly bitter man who downs doubles and waxes vitriolic. At the end of the song, the narrator phones his wife and announces that he's coming home, they're going to work through their problems. I sometimes think I should write an "I met a guy in a bar" song. Mine would be more along the lines of, "I was sitting in a bar and a guy came in and met me."

"Mostly what happens is, Keith will drop an idea on me," Dan-Dan told me. "I'll tape it; it may only last five seconds. Sometimes he'll just sing it to me over the phone. And then I'll go away and work on it for a week or two. We'll get together again and go over it. Finally we'll record it, because you learn things about the song that way. Lyrics that read well don't necessarily sing well, that type of thing."

Danny's forte is lyrics—Danny's forte are lyrics?—but he writes music as well. (He recently co-wrote a song for Dutch singer Anouk, a hit in her homeland, for which his contribution was entirely musical.) How it works—I've grilled him about this mercilessly, trying to see if there isn't a way I could get in on the action—is it becomes generally known within the songwriting community that someone, let's say Josh Groban, is looking for material. "So Josh or someone associated with him will call me and tell me that they're looking," Dan relates, "and then I'll call Keith and maybe a couple of other really talented songwriters I know, and I'll set up appointments for us to get together and write. I concentrate on writing just a few good songs. When I first started, I used to race around and write with fifteen different guys, but it was actually Michael Masser who told me, 'You're crazy. One hit is worth more than any number of near misses. Concentrate on quality.'"

Part of Dan's transformation involved another Don Mills kid, Matt McCauley. Matt was a little younger than me, more of a friend to my brother Joel. Matt's father, Bill, was a musician and a composer, very successful, and Matthew and his brother Tim followed in Bill's footsteps. Matt composed the string parts for Danny's early songs—this is the impression I got—and once they had hooked up with Fred Mollin, whose genius is perhaps of a more maverick nature, there was no stopping them. Matthew and my lovely ex-wife, Dorothy, are also friends, which has to do with a connection to Hamilton, Ontario.

Anyway, the upshot was that Matt McCauley came to visit me at my home. It was a lovely visit, but I had to call it a little short, as I was scheduled to get an X-ray or something at the hospital. Matt kindly offered to give me a lift over there, and as we drove I played him a rough mix of some of the songs I had been working on. Matt listened for a bit, then made me a most amazing offer. "Here's what I'd like to do, Paul," he said. "I'd like you to pick three or four of these songs. I'll write string charts for them, and then we'll record some players down in Nashville. I'll book the studio, I'll hire the musicians..."

It reminded me of the joke wherein a comely woman steps onto an elevator with Donald Trump, declares herself a big fan, and offers to give him a blow job. "What's in it for *me?*" demands Donald.

Bad jokes aside, it was in such a manner that, late last summer, Dan Hill, my brother Joel, and I went to visit the home of country and western music.

WHILE ON the Porkbelly Futures Health Tour, we had passed the Hank Snow Country Music Centre, housed in an abandoned train station near Liverpool, Nova Scotia. As a young boy, when the trains were still running, Hank spent many hours in the station, hiding from an ugly family situation. His parents divorced when Hank was eight—a thing little heard of in maritime Canada, 1922—and he was sent to live with his grandmother, whose lonely house stood on the outskirts of town. Snow's mother moved to Liverpool proper, where she married a man with dark moods and cruel ways. Snow would go to visit his mother, although he was forbidden to do so by his grandmother, and she often beat him on that account. Driven off by his stepfather, he'd be reluctant to return to his gran's, so he'd hide in the train station, caught halfway between two little hells.

So desperate was his situation that Hank put out to sea when he was only twelve years old. One good thing his mother had done was teach the lad how to play guitar, and he took his six-dollar department store instrument (a T. Eaton Special) on board with him. The fishermen on the schooners sometimes received commercial radio signals, and that is how Hank first heard Jimmie Rodgers, the Singing Brakeman. The cabin boy was soon performing "Train Whistle Blues" and "Mother, the Queen of my Heart" for the delighted crew.

A couple of hundred miles up the Nova Scotia coast is Port Hilford, the birthplace, in 1904, of Wilf Carter. When Carter was a boy, a Swiss yodeller passed through town on tour, inspiring little Wilf to become a singer. He left the Maritimes as a young man, travelling to Alberta to work as a lumberjack. He began to entertain out there, largely for the tourists passing through the Rockies. By that time, Carter too had been greatly influenced by Jimmie Rodgers.

Rodgers himself was born in 1897 in Meridian, Mississippi, about twenty miles from the Alabama border. His mother died when he was very small, and Jimmie was sent to live with relatives, sometimes returning to his father's house. His father worked as a brakeman for the railroad. It is the responsibility of the brakeman, as you might infer, to set the brakes; in the early 1900s, the job involved walking along the top of the train while it was in motion, turning a wheel on each individual car. Once he'd grown, Jimmie Rodgers joined his father atop the boxcars. He learned to sing and to strum the guitar by watching his co-workers, who were mostly black and tended to play the blues.

Jimmie caught the performing bug early. He had his own notions of show biz, a combination of minstrelsy and revivalism. Once he took all the sheets from his father's house to fashion a makeshift tent. After his father retrieved him, and whupped his ass for good measure, Jimmie astonished the elder Rodgers by producing enough money to buy new sheets, money he'd earned singing the blues. A few years later, his itinerant career was successful enough that he'd acquired a real tent—but it was lost to a hurricane, and Jimmie went back to working on the trains. He suffered a hemorrhage in his lung and, in the wake of that, contracted tuberculosis. Unfit even to work the railroads, Jimmie chose music as his full-time pursuit, knowing very well he would never earn anything like full-time money from it. Rodgers was a hard-luck guy. That lent his eyes a slightly haunted look, which contrasted with the cocky grin he perpetually wore. This combination of qualities intrigued Ralph Peer, the songcatcher.

In naming Peer a songcatcher, I am differentiating him from someone like Alan Lomax, who was a musicologist. The "catcher" part of the appellation points to the slightly esurient nature of Peer's questing. He was a talent scout, a record producer, mostly in the employ of Columbia and Okeh Records. As such, he recorded what is generally regarded as the first country and western record, "Little Old Log Cabin in the Lane" by Fiddlin' John Carson. In 1927 Peer came to Bristol, Virginia, to hold auditions. He discovered two acts of great significance. One was the Carter Family, who sang a lot of spirituals,[2] and the other was Jimmie Rodgers.

In a somewhat clumsy way, grappling with rhythm, tuberculosis strangling his range down to little more than an octave, Jimmie Rodgers combined black music (the blues) with white (you can't get much whiter than yodelling). Folklore has it that his yodelling was meant to imitate train whistles, but Rodgers often explained it as curlicues he could make with his throat. He claimed to have come upon a show of Swiss Tyroleans and been impressed enough to incorporate the technique into his own act. He used yodelling where a black musician might use a guitar or a harmonica fill. Rodgers also interjected spoken comments. "Good God," he might mutter. In this post–James Brown era, it may appear to us that a white person could never utter "Good God" effectively, but I'm here to assert that Jimmie Rodgers could. He could toss out a "Good God" that contained both despair and hopefulness. Rodgers is often spoken of as the first man to appropriate black music for his own gain. His "Blue Yodel #1"— which we also know as "T for Texas, T for Tennessee"—was one of the first records to sell millions. But whatever spiritual authenticity we might deem necessary to sing the blues, Jimmie Rodgers had it.

Furthermore, Rodgers seems to have conducted himself with a colour-blindness remarkable for the times. Most famously, he recorded with Louis Armstrong in 1930, "Blue Yodel No. 9 (Standing on the Corner)," with Armstrong's wife, Lillian, on piano. Even before that historic event, Rodgers

2 The Carter Family (no relation to Wilf) recorded between 1927 and 1956. The members of the original group were A.P. and Sara Carter and A.P.'s sister-in-law Maybelle. Maybelle's daughter June would go on to perform with, and marry, Johnny Cash.

had cut a side with a black jazz band in Dallas. And neither is Rodgers's influence on black musicians to be ignored. Granted, the best-known of his disciples was white country and western star Ernest Tubb, who more or less dedicated his life to following in Rodgers's footsteps. But there was also Chester Arthur Burnett, a young black kid from White Station, Mississippi. Jimmie Rodgers was Burnett's idol, too, although Chester was undone by a specific inability. "I couldn't do no yodellin'," he recalled later in life, "so I turned to howlin'. And it's done me just fine." Chester Burnett, of course, is the man we know today as Howlin' Wolf.

One of the things that defines country and western music is its instrumentation, which reflects a surprising diversity of influences. The banjo is actually African in origin. The pedal steel is a cousin to the dobro, which was invented and then appropriated by what some people see as opposing camps,[3] deep blues and bluegrass. Both the blues and country and western love the slide, which allows notes to slip into rightness or to go hurtfully flat—which is to say, allows them to sound human. Chord changes are quick but a little bit eerie. Eerie and plaintive.

I know, I know, I've hit upon exactly what you dislike about country and western music, and I am the first to admit that things can go very wrong.

It's true that the music seems to claim more than its fair share of pikers, people with little talent and overly elaborate wardrobes. Sometimes the music makes such a virtue of its honesty that it allows room for rudimentary musical skills and—quite often, in my estimation—vocalizations that lack

3   I don't.

fidelity to pitch. Johnny Cash, for example, could not really sing. He could intone and bellow and execute a passable recitative, but he couldn't sing. I remember watching *The Merv Griffin Show* many years ago. Jazz drummer and noted dickwad Buddy Rich was complaining about the state of popular music, and he selected Mr. Cash for special abuse. Griffin, himself a singer, rushed to Johnny's defence, claiming that Cash sang straight from the heart. "Well," allowed Rich, "he oughtta put the microphone down there, then, because what's coming out of his mouth is crap."

I've been talking classic c&w, but these days what they call "New Country" is all the rage. My teenaged daughter, Flannery, likes New Country, and if the two of us are driving in the car, she will argue that one of the myriad of stations proffering New Country should satisfy us both. She is not entirely mistaken in this. Every fourth or fifth song might prove enjoyable, and given the heavy rotation of the tracks on these stations, some songs become favourites through attrition. After the thousandth time one has heard "Save a Horse (Ride a Cowboy)," one finds oneself nodding in time, mumbling the words through blubbery lips like a broken old prizefighter. But there are also songs I love. Whenever I hear "Probably Wouldn't Be This Way" on the car radio—recorded by LeAnn Rimes, composed by John Kennedy and Tammi Kidd—I feel the need to pull over so that I can blubber unabashedly.[4]

This raises another issue about both New Country and the older stuff: it can be emotionally overwrought, and in the

---

4   This is one of those songs that, like "Ode to Billie Joe," operates on a subtextual level. Oooh, I love subtext. The lyrics demand repeated listening—at least, they did for me, although admittedly I'm not the sharpest knife in the drawer—and will reward the careful listener. And then the careful listener will blubber unabashedly.

wrong hands it is manipulative and maudlin. Listening to an hour or two of New Country, you can start to feel as if you are attending some twelve-step program in which the participants, unhinged from their crutch of dependency, carom wildly from emotion to emotion. "I am a hard-drinking, hard-fighting sumbitch," they proclaim, and not just the men, as Gretchen Wilson fans will know. "I hold certain principles dear, archaic and simple-minded ones, and I do not need to defend them, because I hold them with such conviction that if you question them, I will need to stomp you in the head. On the other hand..." (And I can imagine tears welling now.) "On the other hand, I am the lowliest person who ever trod the earth, and I am undeserving of the love that has redeemed me. The person who loves me..." (it could be parent, partner, or child) "...loves me with a love that is pure and unsullied."

One thing that is certain: it's difficult to get a song played on New Country radio. The gatekeepers seem especially strict. One thing they are patently *not* doing is allowing the previous (and revered) guests to party at the musical mansion. You are not likely to hear Mr. Cash or Dolly Parton or George Jones on these stations. Still, the programmers are deeply suspicious of acts in which people simply don Stetsons and demand a New Country listenership. And a few of the songs are really great songs. This is the market that Dan Hill and his co-writers are aiming for, and every so often they will hit a bull's eye.

THE TRIP I made to Nashville was my version of a pilgrimage to Mecca, and my spiritual needs were taken care of in short order. On our first free afternoon, Dan and Joel and I went down to the Country Music Hall of Fame. There we found on display a glass cloche filled with little pieces of carved wood that formed perches, tables, musical instruments. Stuffed squirrels were arranged around these items so to suggest a quartet: guitar, violin, stand-up, and pedal steel. These squirrels had been killed by Hank Williams.

I don't propose to make fun of this enterprise. To me, the squirrel band seems somehow indicative of Hank's artistry. His songs possess a demographic breadth that is startling, and they have been covered by everyone from Bob Dylan to Perry Como. Here's the thing: I think Hank took his best shot at the human heart, and it's kind of neat that just to the side of misery and gap-toothed exultation (I'm referring specifically to the songs "Your Cheatin' Heart" and "Jambalaya") there is a quartet of dead squirrels.

Death, as you may know, pursued Mr. Williams doggedly. Death was like a truant officer constantly pissed off at this one little kid. You have likely heard the story of Hank's passing, how when his chauffeur pulled the Cadillac into a parking lot somewhere between Knoxville, Tennessee, and Canton, Ohio, on their way to a gig scheduled for New Year's Day, Williams was dead, filled with morphine and painkillers and a lot of booze. It's not as if Hank didn't take a hand in his own passing. Still, when Williams spoke, as he often did, of being pursued by the pale horse and his rider, you had to grant him a little credibility. Hank Williams was just twenty-nine when he died. He had one of those impossibly brief lifespans, like Percy Bysshe Shelley or Franz Schubert.

In my sunnier moods, I remark to myself that I've already managed to nearly double up on those brief existences. (Other times, of course, I am less sanguine. Other times, I glare at elderly people, especially if I catch them drinking, smoking, or eating the wrong foods.) But down in Nashville, Tennessee, it occurred to me that maybe I should do something about making my peace with Forever.

I was also making my peace, let me add, with the here and now. My brother and I were more into food than Danny was, and we spent time exploring some famous local eateries. We engaged a taxi driver to take us to the Loveless Café, which lies some miles southwest of the city proper. Me and Joel[5] and the driver broke fast on country ham, red-eye gravy, and biscuits. Yummy.

In case there is any doubt on the matter, let me state categorically that I like it here. I enjoy the earth and its bounties. I like fishing, I like single malt, I especially like cooked pig in its many manifestations. At the esteemed steak house, Fleming's, we learned once again that, in certain regards, Americans are better than Canadians. Americans know their way around huge slabs of meat, and they certainly know how to handle a great big genetically altered potato. At the Bluebird Cafe, we saw Don Schlitz, the writer of many fine songs. (Including "The Gambler," which just now started playing on the Internet radio station I'm listening to.)

But as those fine days in Nashville ticked away, the thought of preparation seized me. A little phrase came to mind. More an exchange, really.

"Are you ready?"

"Am I ready?"

A call and response, field hands calling back and forth.

"Are you ready?"

With the answer coming, "Am I ready? I believe I am."

5 I know I shouldn't write "me and Joel," but that's what I've been saying all my life.

Danny had instructed the hotel management to put a keyboard in his hotel room, and one morning I walked down the hall and told him my idea. The musical basis for the song, I said, would be the three chords that constitute the underpinning for my song "Mary Cargill." That was the first song I'd ever played for Danny, after our little "Christmas Comes But Once a Year" jape. At the time, Dan-Dan said (without embarrassment or irony, the same way he says everything), "Paul, if I were ever to write a song with somebody else, it would be somebody who wrote a song like that." So I played the three "Mary Cargill" chords in Dan's hotel room and offered my one lyrical notion—it involved a freight train, as many of my lyric ideas do—and Danny took it away. I could see why he is so sought after as a collaborator. He seemed to have endless ideas and very little ego. "Here's what I think, but it doesn't matter to me. I'm just throwing this out there." I am not paraphrasing the general tenor of his input, I am transcribing exactly what he said. And in such a manner was the first verse of our song written.

> The night is coming, creeping oh so close,
> I try to hold it off, but still I know—
> It's like trying to hold back an old freight train
> Coming down on me ... still I'm not afraid
> I've got this feeling that I can't explain
> Like I'm falling through the evening rain,
> Wash me clean before I make my stand
> Are you ready? I believe I am.

I would add more here about the food we ate in Nashville, but it seems a little excessive. Here's my death-defying promise. If I finish this book, and if I subsequently write a little novella, or novelette, or noveleenie, about the early days of gospel music (that's my idea, what do you think, huh, huh?), then I will write a book about all the meals my brother and I ate together. Which, judging from the size of us, were newsworthy and considerable. For now, I will report only that we journeyed back to Toronto and that, two days after our return, both Danny and Joelie called me up to say they missed each other.

As soon as I got home, I went next door and asked Martin to help me with the second verse of the song. His style is different from Danny's, since he tends to shape phrases and sentences fully before he suggests them. We worked away on it, and before long the second verse was complete.

> The ocean is rising as the sun goes down
> What isn't water will surely drown
> But I can't hold the tide at bay
> The moon will rise, it's gonna light my way
> No one can tell me where I'm gonna be
> When I sail into the mystery
> I know I'm falling, don't know where I'm gonna land
> Are you ready? Am I ready? I believe I am.

I had decided on a figure to separate the verses, a simple little march up the fretboard. It suited my musical sensibilities not only to play this figure but to push it suddenly and emphatically up a whole tone, the kind of abrupt key change that characterizes the sweet, soulful Toronto Sound. I played something for Danny and Marty one afternoon in late fall

("We got to finish this thing!"), and Dan started singing some words, being open and confessional.

So close to something, I feel it
All alone, I can't help believing—
Here I go into the Great Unknown

We elected to reprise some of the earlier lyrics, and that was that. The three of us had written a song, and another door thus opens. Dan assures us our song will be a hit. Moreover, it will be a *country* hit. Maybe he's right—who can say? In the meantime, there are plans afoot, more airs and whistles to be fashioned. It ain't over till it's over, and that's good enough, or nearly, for me.

. . .

MARTIN WORTHY *writes:*
The plan had always been to record "Are You Ready" in Nashville. Matt, Fred, and Dan were anxious to get production underway, but first they wanted to hear Paul sing the song himself, as a kind of emotional road map. The easiest thing to do was have him come next door to my little home studio, so that he could record it the way he felt it. I helped him up the stairs that afternoon in early December. Even with the portable O_2 Paul's breathing was laboured, and he was moving slowly. He sat catching his breath for about fifteen minutes while I busied myself adjusting the mic placement and setting levels.

Paul had developed a nagging, random cough that made it difficult to predict how long he could speak or sing without interruption. That, combined with what was by now a constant stream of visitors and phone calls, made us decide to record his guitar and his vocal separately. Laying down the guitar was easy for an old hand like Paul. Despite everything, he then managed an utterly compelling version of the song, straight through, on the second take. We sent the tracks to Nashville, and it wasn't long before Fred and Matt sent back some rough mixes for us to hear. They had kept Paul's simple, achingly honest vocal and surrounded it with the lovingly understated playing of some first-call "Nashville cats." Paul and I sat in his kitchen and listened, gob-smacked.

On a Sunday afternoon in mid-January, Paul and I and our old friend Nick Jennings went to David Gray's studio, where Paul's brother Joel was set to record some bass tracks for Paul's solo record. In his typical style, right as we were packing up, Paul had another idea. "I've got this little tune I'd like to try before we go," he said. Dave scrambled to set up a stereo mic, and Paul encouraged all of us to join him as we recorded it off the floor. It was an old-school way of working, he pointed out, just like in the early days of radio.

Paul referred to himself as "Earl" in the new song; Earl, the leader of a strange band called Earl and the Pearls, was a character he sometimes adopted. Half spoken, half sung, the song charted the evolution of a sign posted on the side of an evangelical church on Richmond Street in Toronto. Paul had been looking at it all his life, and though the format of the sign had changed a few times over the years, the message was always the same: "The End Is Near. Call Jim." Toward the end of the song,

Paul paused for a moment, dialled a number on an imaginary telephone, then joyfully belted out, "Hello Jim! I liked it here! So thanks for telling me that the end is near." Not only was he ready to go, he was letting us know, he had no regrets.

A group of us went out for dinner that night to celebrate Joel's birthday. More friends came over after we got home. We drank wine, laughed and talked about music. Paul died peacefully seventy-eight hours later, on January 21, 2010. He was fifty-six years old.

Hello Jim

I remember when I was a kid, my father would drive me downtown. / This was a long time ago, before the city was anything like the city it is today. / We'd roll down Bayview Avenue and turn on Richmond Street. / And there was this little church there, had a big sign outside. / The sign said, "The end is near. Call Jim. / The end is near. Call Jim."

There was a telephone number. I remember the telephone number. / But I don't think I should tell you what it is. / There seems to be a lot of red tape involved in saying someone's phone number in public. / I will tell you that the number began "Walnut 2." / That's how we said telephone numbers back then: "Walnut 2." "Lennox 3." "Hickory 7." / "The end is near. Call Jim. / The end is near. Call Jim."

I grew up some, and started taking the streetcar downtown. / And sometimes I'd get off at Richmond and walk around a little bit. / And I'd see that church sitting there. / The telephone number was a little different now—"922," it started. / But the message was the same. / "The end is near. Call Jim. / The end is near. Call Jim."

So today, I still live in the city, and sometimes I'll drive downtown. / And I'll take the highway, the super-connector. / And sometimes when I drive past the

Richmond Street exit / I'll peek through the guard rails, and I can see that church. / It's still down there, that little church. / And now the sign says, "www.the end is near.com / www.the end is near.com."

And I need to tell you something else. / The end *is* near. The doctors finished analyzing all the tests they'd given me, / And they said, "Yeah ... the end is near." / They said: "If there are affairs you need to put in order, do so. / If you have unfinished business, you should conduct it. / Because ... the end is near."

I thought about that. / And there *was* one thing I needed to do. / Something I'd needed to do since I was a little boy. / And I picked up the phone ...

"Hello, Jim, my name is Earl!
Lost a lot of fights, got some of the girls.

"Hello, Jim, I enjoyed it here!
Drank too much whisky, just the right amount of beer.

"Hello, Jim. It was a gas.
I like little trouts and big-assed bass!

"Hello, Jim, I liked it here!
Thanks for telling me that the end is near!

"Hello, Jim! Hello, Jim!"

Are You Ready?

The night is coming, creeping oh so close
I try to hold it off, but still I know
It's like trying to hold back an old freight train
Coming down on me... still I'm not afraid
I've got this feeling that I can't explain
Like I'm falling through the evening rain
Wash me clean before I make my stand.
Are you ready? Am I ready? I believe I am.

The ocean is rising as the sun goes down
What isn't water will surely drown
But I can't hold the tide at bay
The moon will rise, it's gonna light my way
No one can tell me where I'm gonna be
When I sail into the mystery
I know I'm falling, don't know where I'm gonna land
Are you ready? Am I ready? I believe I am.

So close to something, I feel it.
All alone, I can't help believing—
Here I go into the Great Unknown

No one can tell me where I'm gonna be
When I sail into the mystery
I know I'm falling, don't know where I'm gonna land
Are you ready? Am I ready? I believe I am.

SOURCES

Brinnin, John. *Dylan Thomas in America*. Toronto: Key
  Porter, 2002.

Brodie, Richard. *Virus of the Mind*. New York: Hay House,
  2009.

Campbell, James. *The Picador Book of Blues and Jazz*. Surrey,
  UK: Picador, 1996.

Cohen, Ronald D., ed. *Alan Lomax: Selected Writings,
  1934–1997*. New York: Routledge, 2003.

Dylan, Bob. *Chronicles: Volume One*. New York: Simon &
  Schuster, 2005.

Moore, Allan. *The Cambridge Companion to Blues and Gospel Music*. Cambridge: Cambridge University Press, 2003.

Palmer, Robert. *Deep Blues*. London: Penguin, 1982.

Shelton, Robert. *No Direction Home: The Life and Music of
  Bob Dylan*. Cambridge, MA: Da Capo Press, 2003.

Solomon, Andrew. *The Noonday Demon: An Atlas of
  Depression*. New York: Scribner, 2002.

PAUL QUARRINGTON was an acclaimed non-fiction writer, novelist, screenwriter, filmmaker, songwriter, and musician. He won the Governor General's Literary Award for Fiction for his novel *Whale Music,* and his last novel, *The Ravine,* was long-listed for the Scotiabank Giller Prize. Quarrington received the Stephen Leacock Medal for Humour for his novel *King Leary,* which was also the victor in Canada Reads 2008. He was frontman, vocalist, and rhythm guitarist for the band Porkbelly Futures.